Listen Linda presents...

The Women of the Waiting Room Surgery for Your Soul

Devotional

**Vessel Jacquiline Cox
and 29 Co-Authors**

The Women of the Waiting Room Devotional

Listen Linda presents...
The Women of the Waiting Room Surgery for Your Soul Devotional

Copyright © 2024 The Women of the Waiting Room Devotional by Pa-Pro-Vi Publishing

Cover Design by Jacquiline Cox

No part of this publication may be reproduced, stored in a retrieval system, or transmitted in any form or by any means, electronic, mechanical, photocopying, recording, or otherwise, without the written permission of the publisher. the only exception is brief quotations in printed reviews.

Pa-Pro-Vi Publishing:
www.paprovipublishing.com

ISBN: 978-1-959667-49-0

*Jacquiline Cox ~ Tracey Adams ~ Dr. Velma Bagby ~ Kecia Boyd
Ivy Caldwell ~ Carolyn Coleman ~ Elizabeth Cotto
Myra Cook ~ Dr. Nakita Davis
Theresa Dorsey ~ Waletta Dunn
Dorian Evans ~ Shana Gourdine
Natashia Hagans ~ Melanie Johnson
Pemela Nance Johnson ~ Charise King
Gwyn Mais ~ Allaina Marie
Dr. AudreyAnn Moses ~ Kimberly Parks
LaQuita Parks ~ Joni Rosebrock
Beverley Rose-Smith ~ Sharon Smith
Sam Marie Thomas ~ Shaday Void
Leticia Perry Warren ~Sandra Washington
Simone Williams*

The Women of the Waiting Room Devotional

Table of Contents

Acknowledgements 5

Foreword Pat G'Orge... 7

Jacquiline Cox... 10

Tracey Adams 22

Dr. Velma Bagby... 28

Kecia Boyd 34

Ivy Caldwell 38

Carolyn Coleman 43

Elizabeth Cotto 49

Myra Cook.. 55

Dr. Nakita Davis 57

Theresa Dorsey 64

Waletta Dunn... 69

Dorian Evans 73

Shana Gourdine 78

Natashia Hagans.. 85

Melanie Johnson 90

Pamela Nance Johnson 96

Charise King.. 101

Gwyn Mais 107

Allaina Marie 112

Dr. AudreyAnn Moses 118

Kimberly Parks 123

Joni Rosebrock 128

Beverley Rose Smith 134

Sharon Smith 141

Sam Marie Thomas 147

Shaday Void 153

Dr. Leticia Perry Warren 155

Sandra Washington 160

Simone Williams 170

LaQuita Parks 176

The Power of Prayer 184

Acknowledgments

I would like to express my heartfelt gratitude to the co-authors of this remarkable anthology, Listen Linda Presents The Women of the Waiting Room: Surgery for Your Soul Devotional. I am incredibly grateful for your acceptance and trust in the vision of God and my call to action. Together, we have taken our stories and allowed them to become vessels to bring more souls to Christ.

I would like to extend my sincerest thanks to the publisher LaQuita Parks, and the Pa-Pro-Vi Publishing team. Your expertise and dedication have helped bring this vision to life.

To all the individuals who have purchased this book, I am deeply grateful for your support. It is because of you that this message can reach those who need it most. I would also like to acknowledge the creatives behind the scenes who have played a crucial role in bringing this vision to fruition. A special thank you goes out to the publicist Dr. Nakita Davis and the Promotional Team MsQueenie Clem for their hard work in spreading the word about this book. Your efforts have not gone unnoticed. I am also grateful for everyone who has liked, shared, or commented positively on the promotional material online. Your support means the world to me.

To my loving husband, Marvis Cox, and my two boys, thank you for standing by me throughout this journey. Your unwavering support and love have been my rock.

Lastly, I want to express my deep appreciation to my sisters in Christ, especially LaQuita "Pa-Pro-Vi" Parks, for collaborating with me in this beautiful ministry to reach others for Christ. Your prayers and encouragement have given me the confidence to press forward. The scripture from Hebrews 10:25 reminds us of the importance of not neglecting to meet together and encouraging one another, especially as the Day draws near.
In the face of limited time, let us be fearless for God. This year, my word is "fearless," and together, let's boldly proclaim His message. I love you all with the love of God.

FOREWORD

Deuteronomy 11:24 Every place where the sole of your foot treads will be yours. Your territory will extend from the wilderness to Lebanon, and from the Euphrates River to the Western Sea. This is Jacquiline Cox. Wherever God leads her success is already waiting. Her faith matches everything about her and it's that which pleases God. The Anthology was already a success from the moment God placed the idea and the participants in her spirit.

The rain falls on the just and the unjust... However, for those in the "Waiting Room" it is a deluge that drowns their fears while watering their hopes and dreams. It is where when the flood of trials begin to ebb and the sun appears; when life's door to hope finally reopens -God sun-bathes them in his blessings. The Waiting Room had become an unknown shelter.

Pat G'Orge

About Pat

Pat G'Orge (pronounced Gee-or-jay) - Walker is in a league of her own. This accomplished Christian author and comedienne has an amazing mind and talent for turning her observations of church life into gems of sidesplitting humor. It is her own special gift from God that enables G'Orge-Walker to depict the often-ridiculous antics of church folk without subverting the Good News or watering down the potency of its message.

Pat G'Orge-Walker has paid a high price for the ever-present smile on her face. This Mt. Vernon, New York PK (preacher's kid) has survived a raging house fire; a violent assault; a car crash that mangled her body and a viral infection that left her temporarily blinded. Through it all, Pat quietly soaked in material from her father's Baptist congregation and her mother's Pentecostal assembly to create the stories that keep readers and audiences howling with laughter.

Pat is a 'kept woman' whose life is held firmly and safely in God's hand. Mercy and compassion season every word spoken or written by Pat, who makes her story palpitate in the hearts of people who readily relate to victory over adversity. The First Lady of Gospel Comedy forges a successful career as author and comedian. She has paved the way for many others in both fields.

Pat's storytelling is likened to Zora Neale Hurston's folklore'a documentation of American culture and church life in literature. National and Essence Bestselling author, Pat G'Orge-Walker, is the creator of the award-winning Sister Betty Christian comedy series published by Kensington/Dafina books.

www.pgorgewalker.com

Wait With Me
Deliverance and Healing in the Waiting Room
Jacquiline Cox

In the waiting room of life, where our souls long for deliverance and healing, we find comfort in the presence of God. Just as Jesus walked alongside His disciples, offering comfort and parables of wisdom, we, too, can seek His guidance and find hope in the metaphorical surgery He performs on our souls. As we wait with faith and trust, let us read the stories of the women in the waiting room and discover the transformative power of God's love.

Scripture: Psalm 25:5 (NIV)

"Guide me in your truth and teach me, for you are God my Savior, and my hope is in you all day long."

Parable of the Sower:

Our souls are like soil in the waiting room, waiting to be cultivated by the Divine Surgeon. Just as a sower scatters seeds, God sows His truth and teachings in our hearts. Let us open our hearts to receive His guidance, allowing His love and wisdom to take root in our souls. As we wait, let us trust that His truth will grow within us, transforming us into vessels of His grace.

Scripture: Matthew 13:23 (NLT)

"The seed that fell on good soil represents those who truly hear and understand God's word and produce a harvest of thirty, sixty, or even a hundred times as much as had been planted."

The metaphor of the Potter:

In the waiting room, our souls are like clay in the hands of a skilled potter. Just as the potter molds and shapes the clay, God molds and shapes us, refining our character and transforming our lives. As we wait for deliverance, let us surrender ourselves to His gentle touch. Trusting His wisdom, He will mold us into vessels that reflect His glory, ready to be used for His purpose.

Scripture: Isaiah 64:8 (NKJV)

"But now, O Lord, You are our Father; We are the clay, and You our potter; And all we are the work of Your hand."

Story of the Bleeding Woman:

In the waiting room, we find inspiration in the story of the bleeding woman who sought healing by touching the hem of Jesus' garment. Like her, we too can approach Jesus with faith, believing His touch can restore and heal our wounded souls. As we wait, let us reach out to Him, trusting that His love and power can bring about miraculous transformation in our lives.

Scripture: Mark 5:34 (ESV)

"And he said to her, 'Daughter, your faith has made you well; go in peace, and be healed of your disease."

Conclusion:

As we wait in the waiting room of life, may we find solace in God's presence. Let us trust in His guidance, surrender to His molding, and reach out to Him in faith for healing and deliverance. Just as the women in the waiting room found hope and transformation, may we, too, experience the surgery of our souls, allowing God to heal, restore, and use us for His glory.

Scripture: Isaiah 40:31 (NIV)

"But those who hope in the Lord will renew their strength. They will soar on wings like eagles; they will run and not grow weary, they will walk and not be faint."

Prayer:

Dear Heavenly Father,

In the waiting room of life, we come before You, seeking deliverance and healing for our souls. Guide us in Your truth and teach us, for You are our Savior, and our hope is in You alone. As we wait, help us to trust in Your wisdom and surrender ourselves to Your gentle touch. Mold us into vessels that reflect Your glory and use us for Your purpose. Just as the women in the waiting room found hope and transformation, may we, too, experience the surgery of our souls, finding solace and healing in Your loving presence. In Jesus' name, we pray. Amen.

May this devotional inspire you to wait with faith and trust, seeking God's deliverance and healing in the waiting room of life. May you find solace in His presence, be transformed by His love, and soar on wings like eagles as you walk this journey with Him.

Surgery 4 Your Soul

In the sacred realm of waiting's embrace,
Where whispers echo and souls find solace,
I weave a tapestry of words and grace,
A poem inspired by the Lord God's trace.

In the depths of the waiting room's domain,
I hear the stories like a gentle rain,
Soothing hearts burdened with sorrow's pain,
A sisterhood of souls, connected, unchained.

With every word, a surgeon's scalpel in my hand,
I mend the wounds, healing the stains that brand,
Metaphors dance like notes of a symphony grand,
Symbolizing hope, transformation, and life's demands.

In this hallowed space, where time stands still,
I feel a presence, a divine power, a thrill,
Guided by grace, surrendering to God's will,
Words pour out, seeking guidance, seeking to fulfill.

Just as Jesus spoke in parables profound,
These words unfold, their meaning unbound,
Inviting contemplation, a journey to astound,
In the waiting room, transformation is found.

Embrace the power of words, both bold and true,
As the Holy Spirit dances through,
Share your stories, your struggles, and breakthroughs,
For vulnerability binds us, making hearts anew.

Reflect on your experiences, let them unfold,
Write them down, let your stories be told,
In vulnerability, find solace, be bold,

Connect with others, in their hands, find hold.

Seek refuge in scriptures, find strength in the Psalms,
Where solace resides amidst life's storms,
And in the Proverbs, wisdom's voice calms,
Guiding us with grace as our souls transform.

Be still, know that God is exalted, divine,
Trust in Him, let your heart and soul align,
Submit to His will, let your path intertwine,
And watch as He makes your journey divine.

In the likeness of God's grace,
I offer this poem a glimpse of this space,
The waiting room, where souls find their place,
And through words, healing and connection embrace.

In the sacred realm of waiting's embrace, I heard the whispers of souls seeking solace. I saw a tapestry of words and grace woven together, inspired by Nikki Giovanni's essence. I felt the power of storytelling and the healing it can bring. And I said a poem, crafted with love and care, to convey a message of hope and transformation.

This experience taught me the importance of sharing our stories, struggles, and breakthroughs. In the waiting room of life, where time seems suspended, we find a sisterhood of souls connected by our vulnerabilities and desires for healing. By embracing the power of words and vulnerability, we can forge deep connections with others and discover solace in our shared experiences.

To apply this message to your life, I encourage you to reflect on your experiences and find the courage to share them. Write them down in poetry or prose and allow your stories to be heard. Embrace vulnerability and connect with others who may be going through similar journeys. In sharing your own struggles and breakthroughs, you find healing for yourself and offer support and inspiration to those around you.

As you embark on this journey of self-expression and connection, I suggest turning to the book of Psalms in the Bible. The Psalms are a collection of poetic expressions that delve into the depths of human emotions, offering solace and guidance.

Psalm 46 is a fitting reading for this message:

"God is our refuge and strength, an ever-present help in trouble. Therefore, we will not fear though the earth give way and the mountains fall into the heart of the sea, though its waters roar and foam and the mountains quake with their surging." (Psalm 46:1-3)

This scripture reminds us that God is our refuge and strength, even during chaos and uncertainty. We need not fear, for His presence is ever-present, offering us solace and guidance. Just as the waiting room can be a place of transformation, so too can our trust in God's unwavering love and support bring about profound change in our lives.

Let us pray:

Dear Heavenly Father,

We come before you today with grateful hearts, acknowledging your presence in our lives. Thank you for the gift of storytelling and the power of words to heal and connect. As we navigate the waiting rooms of life, we ask for your guidance and strength.

Please help us find the courage to share our stories, to be vulnerable, and to connect with others on a deeper level. Grant us the wisdom to see the transformative power of our own experiences and the ability to offer support and inspiration to those around us.

In times of uncertainty and chaos, remind us that you are our refuge and strength. May we find solace in your loving embrace and trust in your plans for our lives. Guide us as we navigate the waiting rooms, and may our journeys be filled with hope, transformation, and a deep connection with you and one another.

In Jesus' name, we pray. Amen.

May this message and prayer inspire you to embrace your stories, connect with others, and find solace in God's unwavering love and presence.

About Jacquiline

Jacquiline Cox is a Chicago native who holds an impressive academic background. She graduated from Dunbar Vocational Career Academy and pursued higher education at Columbia College in Chicago, Illinois. Eventually, she obtained her bachelor's degree in business administration with Cum Laude honors from the University of Arizona Global Campus.

Driven by her passion to make a positive impact on the world, Jacquiline writes to inspire individuals of all genders, races, and ages. She firmly believes that everyone faces challenges in life and aims to provide encouragement through her work. With three published books under her belt, all published by LaQuita Parks of Pa-Pro-Vi Publishing, Jacquiline's literary contributions have been well-received.

But Jacquiline's impact goes beyond the realm of writing. Alongside her husband, she actively engages in motivational speaking engagements at schools and non-profit organizations. Her dedication to empowering others has earned her recognition as a World Record Holder, a member of the NYC Journal's 40 under 40 INNOVATORS: ENTREPRENEURIAL SPIRITS, and a Forbes Blk Member.

With her expertise and accomplishments, Jacquiline is a respected figure in various fields. As a 3-time international best-selling author, branding strategist, and global radio podcast host of Listen Linda!, she uses her platform to motivate and inspire others. Moreover, Jacquiline is an autism parent advocate, a lupus advocate, and a certified Business Coach, showcasing her commitment to supporting causes close to her heart.

In 2017, Jacquiline established Class E Defined, a business venture that offers CryoSkin Services. Her dedication and innovative approach earned her the recognition of the Best New Business in Oswego, IL. During the pandemic, she adapted her business model and diversified her offerings to include digital services. Now, Jacquiline assists clients with marketing and branding sessions, podcast production, content creation, and life coaching sessions.

Overall, Jacquiline Cox's multifaceted journey exemplifies her determination, resilience, and commitment to making a difference in the lives of others.

Find me on social media via Linktree:

https://linktr.ee/youngsavedleaders

Check Your Posture
TRACEY N. ADAMS

Everyone has heard the saying that we must wait on God! Most of us have learned the art of waiting, but what is your posture while waiting on God? Do you wait with a negative attitude? During your waiting process, are you jealous of others who have received their breakthrough? Are you happy for others while you wait? This was me for many years.

At the age of 30, I was married and wanted to have a baby so badly. I thought it was going to be easy, but it wasn't. I suffered several miscarriages, and I was angry at God. I questioned God, asking, "Why do women who don't even want children get to have children?" "Why do women on drugs get to have children?" "Why do women who shack up and are unmarried get to have babies?" I was terrible. I went through counseling, but it didn't help. I just wanted to have a baby! I hated seeing pregnant women. I was invited to several baby showers, and I refused to go because I felt like it was a slap in my face. I cried incessantly. I didn't talk to my husband or my family for that matter. I just went to work and came home and cried!

While waiting for God to come through, I felt sorry for myself. I could not be happy for others. I was jealous and did not congratulate them. This made waiting very difficult for me. I had to wait longer than I was supposed to. It seemed like my breakthrough would never come. After 5 years, God blessed me with a beautiful and healthy baby girl! Four years later, He gave me another beautiful baby girl! I was very grateful, and I felt extremely blessed! The Holy Spirit checked me, and I had to fall on my face in tears and repent to the Father for my posture while I waited on my miracles.

Fast forward to the here and now, I listen to a preacher whose ministry is based in another state. One morning, while getting ready for work, I was listening to one of his sermons, and he asked the question, "What is your posture while you wait on God?" He talked about everything I had experienced while waiting for God to bless me with a baby. He said that although many of us have mastered waiting, how we wait and our posture, while we wait, hinders many of our blessings. The blessing is coming. God heard you, but you must have the correct posture while waiting. That word was confirmation for me. What I learned the most about waiting is being happy for others when they receive their blessings and genuinely congratulate them.

I am waiting on God for a financial miracle to become debt-free. While I wait, I will be happy for others and celebrate their breakthrough. I am waiting for God to heal my body from hip surgery. While I wait, I continue to pray for healing for others. I want to be married again. Not just married but in a happy marriage to a man who has been praying for a woman exactly like me. While I wait, I pray for marriages and congratulate engagements and anniversaries. Remember, it's not just waiting; it's your posture while you wait.

Check your posture.

About Tracey

Tracey Nicol Adams was born in Kansas City, MO and is the youngest of seven children. She moved to Atlanta, GA in 1994 to attend and eventually graduate from the prestigious Morris Brown College. She has been an elementary and special needs teacher for 24 years. Tracey began writing stories as a child and started keeping journals while in college. She has always wanted to be an author. She has read a plethora of books over the years from various authors and always thought to herself, "I can do this!"

Due to school, marriage, career, children, divorce, and just…life, Tracey put writing on the back burner for nearly 20 years. She began writing again in 2016 and decided that one day she was going to become a published author. She wrote her first book in March of 2016. It is called <u>Maya and the Ants</u> and it's a story about her oldest daughter and how she reacts to her baby sister inviting ants to live in their house. In late November 2016, after her college track coach passed away, Tracey started writing her second book, a realistic fiction novel called *While I Run This Race*.

Tracey's first book was published in 2022 and is currently live and available for purchase. It is entitled *How William Got His Wings.* she was initially going to collaborate with William and call it *William's Journey* but unfortunately William gained his wings before starting the project. With permission from William's dad, Tracey wrote *How William Got His Wings* soon after William's passing in July 2022. A portion of the proceeds from the book goes to his family to honor his memory.

During the time that William was sick and later transitioned, Tracey's mother was also sick, and she passed away 2 weeks after William. While mourning William and her mother, the sequel, *How William Met Mommy*, was birthed.

Her current projects are *How William Met Mommy* and *Too Much of a Good Thing: A Runner's Journey*. They are currently in the illustrating and editing process.

Tracey is extremely excited about this journey in her life and career. She is establishing her book distribution platform and business: TNA Literary Works Presents. Her goals are to share her stories while encouraging various audiences. Tracey wants to write screenplays and TV series based on her realistic fiction books.

For more information about Tracey's books and upcoming

projects, visit her site at:

https://sites.google.com/view/tna-literary-works/home

Keep Your Head Up Princess
DR. VELMA BAGBY

Keep Your Head Up, Princess came from a place I didn't know existed. As I began writing, the story of my experience during my early years, which remained hidden all these years, flowed from my heart onto my manuscript. In writing it, I recognized for the first time what my parents were attempting to pour into me. My journey of how it became increasingly difficult to hold on to my value and worth as I walked through the attacks that sought to minimize it, from the age of eleven years old until I turned twenty-four years old.

I pray my story encourages you to do the same.

When I committed my life to the Lord at age 24, my life left the past attacks on my worth and value and embraced what my parents and God said. I have not looked back since that moment.

Here are a few things I want to share with you about God. God put me in the right place, with the right family, the right financial status, the right neighborhood, the right school, and the right situation, to birth forth what He preordained and orchestrated to occur in my life. God knew every aspect of the disappointments, hurt, judgment, and worldview designed to chip away at my value and worth.

One would ask, why would a loving God allow such things? I was told once that God loves creating testimonies. There are no testimonies without a test. But I also discovered that God didn't need me, I needed Him! I could not find him if I believed I could face life alone. Well, I couldn't. I discovered I was never alone. I had to acknowledge the God of all creation who was there the entire time. God was waiting for me to reach out and find Him. He was right there, ready to meet my needs, not me meet His. I could not negotiate with God on what I preferred as the route I should have taken to find Him. Of course, I would have chosen an easier path.

God preordained the moment I completely embraced who I was and am in Him. I first recognized that I am His chosen vessel, ordained before the foundation of this world, His special creation, and the answer to a problem that "was not good," he created me—the woman to be the good concerning man. I'm joint heirs with Jesus Christ, the Son of the living God. I'm holy royalty, the daughter of the most High God, and the possessor of heaven and earth. Now, that's value. That's worth. Woman, you are all these things and more. YOU are worthy! Invite God in, and let Him give you all you need to embrace who He created you to be.

Acts 17:24-25 ESV says, "The God who made the world and everything in it, being Lord of heaven and earth, does not live in temples made by man, nor is he served by human hands, as though he needed anything since he himself gives to all mankind life and breath and everything."

About Dr. Velma

Award-Winning/Bestselling Author / Certified Dating-Relationship Coach / Ordained Minister (ThD) /

CEO, Adoni Publishing, LLC

Using Biblical principles to help women date4marriage, fall in love with God and embrace their worth.

Love made possible. John 3:16

Dr. Velma is an Award-Winning, Bestselling Author. She published 17 books, with two currently on pre-order.

She wrote her first book, encouraged by her adult daughters, a Christian nonfiction relationship-focused book based on their conversations about men. It became a call to action for single Christian women to date with intent. Inspired by her blessed marriage of 49 years, Dr. Velma continues her focus on dating & relationships, using the storytelling style of Jesus. Jesus wrote over 50 parables/fiction stories, and they included an item familiar to the listener, a connection allowing the listener to see themselves in it, redemption and it was the listener's choice to change in the end. His stories were non-threatening and never preachy. Dr. Velma found Christian Contemporary Fiction a genre perfect for sharing Christian principles that can appeal to those who aren't familiar with scripture—whether in the church or outside of it.

She applies this storytelling style in *The CATCH Series,* where she uses fish analogies to show the dating mistakes of the character: the catfish who loves garbage, the sturgeon who likes to nibble, the salmon who refuses to get caught, and the pufferfish who is handsome until agitated. The book garnered rave responses from book promoters, podcasters, and readers who saw themselves in the stories and met men like the fish characters. Responding to the readers' request for more fish analogies, the novel is now a 4-book series. Book #4 is in response to her male readers, who asked about the wrong women to date, The WRONG CATCH – She'll Tear Down the House.

A Certified Christian Dating-Relationship Coach and a member of the American Association of Christian Counselors (AACC), Dr. Velma has 30+ years of ministering to women and provided pre-marriage and marriage counseling with her husband. A seasoned Women's Ministry Leader, she enjoys explaining scriptures to teach others. Her popular speaking topics are: *Dating4Marriage, How to Avoid Dating a Fool, using Conditions vs Characteristics when dating, Declutter-Lay Aside Every Weight,* and *The Woman in the Mirror.*

She is a wife of Pastor Bruce. The two have two daughters, three grandchildren and a writing buddy, Gracie the German Shepherd.

https://linktr.ee/drvelma

This is my Testimony
KECIA BOYD

My waiting room testimony has been financial, medical, and wanting to change jobs. Times were very hard a couple of years ago. I was trying to figure out how to stay afloat in this economy, experiencing a few medical challenges, and wanting another job. I didn't see a way out. Maybe I wanted too much at one time. I tend to stress myself by overthinking and wanting things to happen all at once.

Patience is very hard for me, so a couple of years ago, I was struggling financially and trying to figure out what to do to make things happen. I knew that a career change was one thing that needed to happen. Trying to navigate that was very hard in the beginning. I was applying for jobs, and nothing was coming my way. I was getting frustrated and feeling it wasn't meant for me.

The jobs I was offered were not a good fit, and when they did sound good, something in the back of my mind told me this was not it. I do believe that God told me everything that sounds good is not good.

There was a time when I decided to stop looking and stay where I was. Now, I am stressing even more because I haven't been successful with a new full-time or part-time job, so it was time to make sacrifices and cut back on things that were not that important or necessary.

Changes were made, and I had to make it work, and for a while, it did. I also started experiencing some female issues and went to see my OB/GYN to explain to her what happened. She decided that a biopsy needed to be done first, and that word scared me a lot, but all I could do was pray. Thank God everything was good.

Life is strange. The minute you let something go, then you get the call. I had forgotten how many jobs I had applied for. Although I was getting calls, I still waited for something good to come through. I really wanted a work-from-home job, but the pay was not it. One morning, I received a phone call from one of the positions I had applied to and had genuinely forgotten about, asking if I was still interested in the position I applied for; of course, I said yes. It was at an outpatient rehab clinic as a scheduler. I was excited about it, and, for once, I felt good about this interview.

The interview went well, and I put it in God's hands. If it's meant to be, it will be. When I tell you, God showed up for me. It was probably a month after the interview when I received the phone call asking if I wanted the position, and I accepted. It showed me that even though we think he is not paying attention or listening to us, He is, and things happen in his time, not ours. All the jobs I didn't get or had a not-so-good vibe were not the jobs for me. He answered my prayers, and he showed up for me. Now, I pay attention to his timing, and most of all, I am learning how to have patience because I know He's got me.

This is my Testimony!

About Kecia

Kecia Boyd was born in Atlanta, Georgia but raised in Dekalb County with her mom, stepdad, and siblings. Her family and her friends have always been important to her. Along with being outside playing kickball, football, and baseball with friends from the neighborhood, she loved to read.

She realized early in her life that she had a passion for taking care of people. Kecia ended up going into the medical field. Even though Nursing was her first thought, she ended up taking care of patients and being a unit secretary.

Kecia has always wanted to be an author and this is her first book. She loves music, reading, watching sports and cooking. Kecia lives in College Park, Georgia. Connect with Kecia on Facebook at https://www.facebook.com/chellbrownsugar

The Women of the Waiting Room Devotional
Waiting For the Restoration of My Soul
Ivy Caldwell

When you think about the waiting room in a hospital, you are not there because you want to be there. You are there because you want answers about what is happening in your body or in support of someone you know. As you wait, you begin watching those who are already there waiting, those who are coming in, and those who are leaving. Those who have been there for some time are getting anxious, and you wonder how long they have been waiting. You wonder how long you will have to wait. You begin watching the clock constantly, and so much time has gone by that you can't believe you are still sitting there waiting. Everyone is in pain and waiting to be seen by the doctor or nurse. It doesn't matter who calls your name because all you know is that you are ready for the pain to stop. You want to know what is going on so that you can leave. The last thing you want is to be checked into the hospital. As in life, the waiting season of the restoration of our soul is a part of our journey to wholeness.

The waiting room chairs are uncomfortable. You are sitting there in pain and wish they would hurry up and call your name. You are anxiously waiting to find out what is the diagnosis of your condition. You may have an idea about what is going on within your body, but you aren't completely sure, so you want to hear from the expert. As in life, our emotional pain is uncomfortable. We may know what the problem is but we have been putting it off as we do in the natural until we can no longer bear the pain of it all. We can only ignore what we have experienced for a season, and sooner or later, we will have to get to the real reason for the emotional pain. We come face to face with the root of the matter, dig it up to process it, and become free of it.

As I sit here and think about my personal waiting room experiences, I have been waiting for years for the emotional pain to end. A waiting room can also symbolize a holding station. This means you aren't ready yet to move forward because you are stuck in this place of holding. God had me in this place of waiting for Him to call my name and open doors so that I could be seen by the Great Physician. As long as I think I can do life, ministry, family, or business in my strength without dealing with the emotional pain, I will be waiting until I realize that I need God in my stuff. God is the one who has given me this life, family, ministry, and business. It will take God to shift things in my mind, soul, and life to move forward as He has already planned and designed for it to go.

The waiting seasons of my life were necessary for my development and maturity in God. It was a period of growth and learning about who I am in God. The waiting room of experiences has shaped my life into who I am today. I had to sit in the waiting room of life and look within myself to see what areas needed healing. I had to wait to get an understanding, get the proper knowledge about why it happened, and wait to get answers to my questions from God. God did the work in me so I can, in turn, help those who are in the waiting stage of life. There comes a time when we must do something to allow God to restore our souls. We must put ourselves in a place of submission and position for the Great Physician to do His work in our lives.

Waiting for the Great Physician to show up on the scene to give me my diagnosis and prognosis was worth the wait. I was bound, but now I am free and made whole again. My years of waiting have been for the emotional healing of my soul. I am an overcomer of childhood sexual trauma, and it has taken me many years to get to a place of healing. I don't know exactly when it happened. All I can tell you is that God is a healer, and He has restored my soul. He has turned my mourning into joy and dancing. I give God all of the praise, glory, and honor.

I have been waiting to see victory in my life, not realizing that I already had victory. It was all part of my plan written in the book. God has some good news for you, too. He is waiting to restore your soul.

About Ivy

Ivy Caldwell is a wife of over 30 years, a mother of 4 sons, a grandmother of many,

A 33X author, a 13X bestselling author, an international author, a children's book series publisher, an international speaker, a certified empowerment life coach, an ordained Elder, a community chaplain, and a T.V. and podcast host. She is CEO/Founder of Footprint Enterprises, which serves women and youth suffering in silence from trauma through her coaching program called "Stepping Into ANEW You."

Through empowering and transforming their minds through the Word of God to expose their T.R.U.T.H. by taking a leap of faith to walk into a confident, bold freedom of wholeness and restoration to embrace all of whom God has created them to be by becoming ANEW You! No longer sit in mute agreement with fear, shame, guilt, hurt, anguish, and humiliation. She dares you to "Expose It!" and "Step Into ANEW You.

Healing For The Soul
CAROLYN COLEMAN

I often think of the woman with the issue of blood; she saw physician after physician, but no one could heal her. She saw Jesus and knew if she could just touch the hem of His garment, she would be made whole; she did, and she was. Talk about the faith of mustard seeds. Jesus felt virtue leave Him and wanted to know who touched Him. She was afraid and owned up to the act. He told her that her faith had made her whole. ***Luke 8:43-48. KJV***

We can also ask for wholeness when we are broken or sick. He still performs miracles. We just need to have faith.

Our God is a miracle-working God; he still performs miracles daily. There is nothing too hard for Him.

God heals the brokenhearted and binds up our wounds. ***Psalms 147:3 KJV***

For He is Jehovah Rapha, the God who heals. ***Psalms 30:2 KJV***

The word of God tells us that by His stripes, we are healed. ***Isaiah 53:5 KJV***

Utilize healing scriptures when praying for healing; pray God's word to Him, not that he has forgotten; we are praying His word over who and where the healing will occur. That speaks of your trust and faith in God. **Psalm 12: 6-7 KJV. Psalms 103: 3**

When praying for healing, pray in faith that the healing has occurred. We walk by faith, not by sight.

Declare and decree that you are healed. The Lord directed us to speak those things that are not as though they are. Healing needs can range from dealing with low self-esteem and anxiety to healing for your physical or mental health. Relax in your healing season, seek therapy, and get a massage. It is therapeutic to walk, eat healthy meals, and get enough sleep. Stress can delay your healing process.

When praying for someone who is having surgery, pray for the patient, the surgical team, and the surgeon.

Acknowledge who God is. Lord God Jehovah, you are the Great I AM (Exodus 3: 14 KJV). You can do anything but fail. God loves his children. He has an expectant end for us, and that is to prosper us and not to harm us.

Not all food is prepared the same way, and various temperatures are used. No one can tell you when you are healed. Individually, we heal at different times. Go to God in prayer; seek his deliverance and healing for you. You will heal in your time. This may be your night season, but the day comes in the morning. Remember to forgive the person who hurt you. Once you are healed, you are stronger. Accept what once was and move forward.

Things to know or do to promote your healing.

Pray

Forgive yourself.

Forgive the one who hurt you.

Journal your feelings.

You are enough.

No, it is a complete sentence.

You are Beautiful.

Celebrate You

You are worthy,

Love yourself.

Protect your peace.

Avoid negativity.

Self-care

Everyone can not join you on your healing journey; they are there for the show.

Do not date or enter a relationship during your healing process.

About Carolyn

Carolyn Pickens Coleman is a daughter, wife, mother, sister, cousin, friend, and co-worker from Bessemer, Alabama. She has a B.S. in Nursing from Samford University and an M.A. in Health Service Administration from Strayer University. Carolyn is an active member of the Birmingham Black Nurses Association, Inc., and served as the Chairperson of the Outreach committee for two years and is the current President of the Bessemer Public Library Trustee Board, She is also a Board Member of C.H.L.M.S. Medi-Helpz Foundation whose mission is Patient Engagement, Empowerment as well as education for the patient and community.

Carolyn has more than 37 years of experience as a critical care nurse and presently a nurse case manager. She worked with hospital administrators to establish plans regarding complex patient cases, concentrating on outcome management, utilizing best practices, advocating for patients. She is also an adjunct instructor.

Carolyn is the author of a five-book series. The title character is Gentry who faces her life choices, as we all do, For Carolyn, writing is cathartic. She enjoys reading and staying active by line dancing, walking, and spending time with her family and friends.

Carolyn has co-authored two #1 Best-selling anthologies, one was also an international best seller.

A Warrior Mermaid Can Overcome Storms
ELIZABETH COTTO

Hello, my name is Elizabeth Cotto, and I am thirty-nine years old. I birthed two boys, and I consider eight other children/young adults like they are my own. I consider myself a Warrior/Mermaid. (LOL)

This is my testimony and part of my life story. Before I share part of my story, I want to share this quote I read in a Facebook group on my page called "Quotes for the Human Experience." After I had read that quote, I felt so emotional because I realized I had been that girl in the quote for many years, even as a young child. The quote read,

"To the girl who hasn't been herself lately:

Your spark will return, and you will shine like you were meant to.

It's difficult when you catch yourself not being you.

When you feel your whole world falling apart before your eyes."

You see, at that moment, I realized I had always been in the waiting room, even as a young child. I am sure many of you can also relate. At that very moment, even though I felt so many different emotions, from feeling sad, disappointed, worthless, a failure, and alone, I also felt my heavy heart disappearing slowly. This happened because I began to pray from the bottom of my heart and finally put all my worries in our Lord's hands without being upset with him.

I finally did what my mom, my three best friends, my two cousins, my two therapists, and my psychiatrist/psychologist have been advising me for years. It felt great; I began to feel less stressed and less worried, I did not feel worthless or a failure, and most importantly, I did not feel alone. I felt our Lord's presence near me. I thought, "Why did you wait so long to take this step?" I think it took me this long to take this step because of all the struggles and bad situations I went through since my childhood. I have always had trust issues, I am an over-thinker, and I have always focused on the negative things and not the positive things in life. Honestly, I am still working to change those things about myself.

I will begin by sharing one of my recent testimonies that shaped my life, how I overcame finding the strength in God's love, and how I witnessed the miracles that unfolded within me while in the waiting seasons of my life. The last relationship I was in lasted 4 years. I truly loved him with all my heart and soul. I never had such an amazing, loving, caring, dedicated, responsible, faithful, and loyal man. He was the greatest and nothing like my boys' fathers.

Unfortunately, at the end of August 2022, I began going through the worst experience of my life. My entire world shattered into trillions of little pieces. On that day, a few days after my birthday, the love of my life left my children and me when we needed him the most. I felt like the world ended for me. I went into the worst depression I had ever faced in my life. Mind you, I have dealt with deep depression since I was a child, but this time, it was the worst.

I couldn't function at all. I did not have the desire to do anything I used to love doing, like cooking, cleaning, and doing my hobbies; I couldn't even listen to any music or even read my bible. Those who know me well know I love listening to music all day. I also love dancing, singing, and doing my nails and hairstyles. I could no longer go on adventures like fishing, going to the beach, or driving to various places in Florida with my family. I wasn't even able to attend church. I lost about 50 pounds within weeks, and I couldn't sleep or eat at all. I was in excruciating pain and in the most horrible, deep depression I have ever faced.

I began struggling with everything, including with my children. Both of my boys are special needs children; despite their multiple conditions, they are both so intelligent and achieve their goals, but they too were in the same depression I was in; they began blaming themselves for the reason why my ex left us. My boys considered my ex the best father figure they have ever had. They considered him their dad, or as they call him, "Pops." To this very day, they still consider him their Pops. I had to speak to them and assure them that it wasn't their fault. The reason why he had to leave was because he had a mental breakdown due to all the struggles we were facing. He felt like he had failed us, and he didn't want to continue hurting us.

My boy's grades began to drop at school. I ended up getting them a therapist and getting myself one as well because I was in this horrible state of depression literally for close to two years. I prayed and prayed but felt it wasn't working for me. I had given up and seriously did not want to live anymore. I felt that there was no reason I should be alive. I was extremely upset with our Lord. I kept saying why did you allow this to happen if you were the one who brought him to my life and my boy's lives. I felt this way for so long, but despite how upset I was with our Lord, I kept praying and praying.

Finally, in December of 2023, before Christmas, I woke up on a Friday morning feeling happy, energetic, and hopeful. I wanted to organize my entire home, deep clean my whole apartment, and I felt like listening to music again, and reading the bible, so that is exactly what I did. Since that day, I have been happy and satisfied with myself, desiring and having the energy to accomplish all my goals despite my severe health conditions. I am grateful and blessed to have the Lord with me all the time. I have dedicated myself to our Lord once again. I also feel thankful to have all the amazing people (and you know who you are) by my side, helping, praying, and pushing me to fight through that horrible battle I was facing. I love you all so much.

I am still learning, but I have so much faith that I know the Lord is helping me through it. Thank you all for taking the time to hear my testimony. I am another living example that God is great all the time; we just have to trust him and dedicate our lives to him. I recently came across this verse, and I loved it. I want to share this with you all. I also want to end my testimony with this Bible verse.

In Isaiah 40:31, the word says, "They that wait on the Lord will renew their strength; they will mount up with wings like the Eagles."

About Elizabeth

Elizabeth Cotto was born and raised in the city of Chicago. She is also Puerto Rican. She now resides in Florida. She has lived in Florida for six years and she loves it. When she lived in Chicago she worked as a Credit Investigator at a loan company, she then became a teacher with children from six weeks old to five years old.

When she moved to Florida, she received her Security license and became a Security Officer. This field in law enforcement, has always been one of her passions in life. Another passion of Elizabeth is that she loves to sing, dance, fish, help others in need, go on adventures with her family. She loves spending time with her family.

She is actively involved with her Church Community; she also loves to listen to "Listen Linda". Elizabeth is a single mother of two boys and she also has four girls and six boys that she considers her own children as well. They are all her strength to continuing to achieve all her goals.

My Waiting Room Testimony
MYRA COOK

You know how you always ask, "Lord, why me, why me?" And you hear the answer, "Why not you?"

That's what I felt when I found out that I had narcolepsy and that there was no cure.

I told my parents in 1975 that I finally found out what was wrong with me. I was diagnosed with narcolepsy. I was so relieved.

My father said, "Oh, I have that, and my daddy had it."

"And you're just now telling me this?"

His answer was, "We just thought you were lazy."

Lazy, how could that be? You have a child who slept all the time, and you didn't think that was odd and did not take me to a doctor. How could that be?

After that announcement, I needed to know more about narcolepsy. I stayed at Erlanger Hospital's library, discovering everything I could about this disease.

The first thing I needed to know was if there was anyone else out there suffering from narcolepsy. I put an ad in a local weekly newspaper asking if anyone had narcolepsy-cataplexy syndrome to contact me (I gave my work number).

Boy, there were lots of people that had narcolepsy, or they had a sister or knew someone with it. Men were dishonorably discharged from the military.

After forming a support group through Memorial Hospital, we joined The Narcolepsy Network. They supplied us with pamphlets and information needed to maintain a normal life. It wasn't easy living with narcolepsy and all of the secondary symptoms that were associated with the disease. Most people didn't believe it was an actual disease.

Everywhere I went, I talked about narcolepsy to someone. I did newspaper interviews, and our local black radio station, WNOO, interviewed me; Channel 9 and Channel 12 also interviewed me. I needed to get the word out about narcolepsy.

God gave me a platform to reach and teach others about narcolepsy. The personnel for the company I worked for told me that I didn't have to tell anyone who interviewed me for a job about me having narcolepsy, but I didn't feel right not letting them know in advance about my condition. I wasn't raised like that, and I wouldn't be a true Christian to lie about it. I lost many in-house interviews, but at least I was honest.

I could not understand why I couldn't get a job as a secretary; I was more than qualified, and that was what I went to college for. I was a fast typist, I could take shorthand at 100 words per minute, I was secretary to my church and class secretary, and I took great notes. I couldn't understand it. I was taking medication for narcolepsy so I could work. Then one of my Preacher friends said, "Maybe that wasn't what God wanted you to do?" It never occurred to me to even put God in what I wanted for my life. From then on, I never applied for a secretary position; I was content with what I was doing.

Why me, Lord, I had once asked him. Now I know why me. He knew that I could handle whatever he dished out to me. I noticed that this has made me a stronger person. Growing up, I was shy; I didn't know how to talk or relate to people, but now I can hold my own with anyone.

I've learned to trust him, and God gets all the glory through my story!

About Myra

Myra, a seventy-two-year-old retiree, embarked on a new chapter in life after a fulfilling 36-year career as an intake specialist. Inspired by her love for reading and interactions at multiple Christin Book Lovers Retreats (CBLR), she delved into writing as a first-time author for this anthology project.

A woman of unwavering faith, Myra actively serves as a church secretary at Quinn Adams Community Church. Her personal journey with narcolepsy-cataplexy syndrome since 1975 fuels her passion to raise awareness about the condition emphasizing its hereditary nature and the importance of effective management.

Despite her challenges, Myra continues to advocate for living life to the fullest. Blessed with two adult children, three grandchildren and two great-granddaughters, Myra cherishes her family and strives to make a positive impact through her writing and advocacy efforts.

The Mighty Middle
DR. NAKITA DAVIS

"But seek first the kingdom of God and his righteousness, and all these things will be added to you." Matthew 6:33 ESV

The world encourages us to celebrate the victorious moments of life, the highs, and cherish the mountaintop peaks. This is when we are told we will feel most abundant. Only when we experience times of struggle, grief, uncertainty, or despair are we advised to pray and seek higher guidance.

Through my experiences as a devoted wife, mother of two wonderful children, successful entrepreneur of two global businesses, and a Woman after God's own heart, I have learned that I don't need to wait for a victory to praise the Lord for His goodness, His abundance, or my blessings. I can praise Him right now - in the midst of it all.

Even in times of doubt, when things seem uncertain or not going as planned, I don't have to wait for despair, gloom, and doom to seek God's presence and PRAY. His wisdom, love, and grace are more than enough for me on my good days, *not-so-good days,* and everything in between.

Reflecting on how Christ's love has guided me through the toughest times and victories fills my heart with sincere gratitude. The journey, not just the destination, matters.

It will always be the "journey" for me.

While we often rush towards our goals, seeking *God's Divine timing* and then **BOLDLY** Acting in obedience to His instructions will lead to an abundant life in Him. My sincere hope is that as you wait, even in the *land of the middle,* you find reasons to praise God for all He has done, all He is doing, and all He has in store for your life!

Waiting while seeking His face is never a chore or punishment; but a perfect time to surrender all to Him for your BEST and BRIGHTEST Days Ahead.

Prayer

Read This Prayer Aloud and with Authority

Heavenly Father,

I Thank you in advance for this Divine opportunity to sit still and rest at your feet. Today, I choose to rest my thoughts and mind and any anxiety, worry, fear, or strife.

I recognize that You alone are God. You are the Alpha and Omega. And You make NO Mistakes.

In this uncertain season of my life where I am unsure of my next move, I willfully give my thoughts over to you. I give my ways and strategic planning over to you. I freely align myself with only the people, places, and things that delight you!

Today, I seek first the Kingdom of God and your Righteousness.

You said in Your word that ALL things will be added unto me, and I believe you.

I know that my flesh desires to move faster, accelerate abundance quicker, and skip over all the obstacles in my way.

Instead of following my desires, I only desire the very BEST that you have in store for me at the precise time you make it available to me!

Help me get into position, stay in position, learn, and grow with the wisdom and discernment required to truly live an abundant life pleasing to you.

Help me to be patient when it is necessary and ready to go when you say MOVE!

I love you, I praise you, and I thank you!

In the matchless name of Jesus Christ

Amen!

About Dr. Nakita

Dr. Nakita Davis is a PR Guru, Celebrity Media Correspondent, Powerhouse Global Influencer, Keynote Speaker, Award-Winning Publisher, and 24x National/12x International Bestselling author.

Dr. Davis is a Presidential Lifetime Achievement Award recipient, 40 Under 40 Lister named by NYC's Journal, an Inaugural AT&T Dream in Black Honoree, and a proud member of ForbesBLK - a platform of Forbes, compiled of Elite Black and Brown professionals crushing glass ceilings and breaking down barriers for people of color.

Additionally, she is an active (BES) member of the Black Excellence Society. She is the CEO and Founder of Jesus, Coffee, and Prayer Christian Publishing House LLC and the CEO of the Women Win Network, where she celebrates Women Who Win 365 via her Television network, global digital magazine publication and curated Exclusive VIP Experiences.

Her platform expands into Hosting POP Your Crown, Sis! Podcast- reaching over 700 million devices via IHeart Radio, Pandora, Apple, Spotify and more.

Dr. Nakita Davis has been featured/seen with FORBES, BET, MTV, ABC, NBC, CBS, FOX, and countless reputable publications and billboards. She resides in Atlanta, GA, with her loving husband and their 2 beautiful children.

Follow on

IG/FB @jesuscoffeandprayer

IG @WomenWinNetwork

Visit online: www.jesuscoffeeandprayer.com

PR/Media opportunities Email: Info@jesuscoffeeandprayer.com

Our Way or God's Way
THERESA DORSEY

Psalms 119:105 NIV – Your word is a lamp for my feet, a light to my path.

In the trials of life, we're faced with two paths: our way and God's way. Our way may seem like the right way initially, but it can be riddled with unnecessary pain and grief. God's way is smooth and easy if we believe Him for our guidance. Being human isn't always easy. We're constantly making decisions that affect our lives for good or bad. We're tempted by money, lust, and power in a world that makes us feel powerless. We're driven by desires, by wants, by passions. But how do these things align with our walk with God and his desires for our lives?

Finding our footing in life is hard. We're constantly tested, trying our best to be decent humans in a world of selfishness and greed. Life wasn't meant to be a cakewalk, but the beauty of God's promise is that we always have a choice. We choose to be obedient. We choose to be good. We choose to be faithful. We choose to be servants of the Lord. We choose to give honor and praise for the blessings we've received and the blessings we've yet to come. But what happens when we slip up? What happens when we fail to follow the path that God has laid out for us? The answer is simple: we can choose to repent. We can choose to be redeemed. God understands that we may sometimes fall short of His glory, but He allows us to come back to His love, be embraced in His arms, and be made whole again.

This verse in Psalms tells us that God's word will light the path to Him and that if we follow the path diligently and without fail, we won't be led astray. With so many temptations and distractions today, God's love never fades. His light never diminishes, even in the middle of the darkest storm; He is ever-present. His light shines on our confusion, bringing us clarity. His light shines on our heartache, bringing us peace. His light shines on our hearts, giving us unconditional love and acceptance. He only asks that we stay on the path of righteousness He has set before us. When the winds of life attempt to blow you in a different direction, use His light to guide you.

About Theresa

Theresa Dorsey is a multi-award-winning author of contemporary women's fiction. An avid reader from an early age, she began her journey as a novelist on a dare from a high school friend, penning her first book at the tender age of 16.

Theresa boldly proclaims that storytelling is her superpower. Writing under the pseudonym Reese, she released her debut novel, Trapped, in June 2022.

She is currently working on the second installment of The Trapped Series entitled Released and is also pursuing her master's degree in English and Creative Writing at Southern New Hampshire University.

Beyond The Comparison Trap
WALETTA DUNN

Have you ever wanted something so bad you would do just about anything to get it? That's how my husband and I felt when we decided to enlarge our family. God had blessed us with a beautiful baby girl. When she was six years old, she asked us for a baby brother. Undenounced to her, we'd asked God for a second child. Specifically, a boy named Michael. *"And all things, whatsoever ye shall ask in prayer, believing, ye shall receive."* **Matthew 21:22 KJV**

Both my husband and I grew up with siblings in the house. We enjoyed the privilege of having someone to play with, to share your secrets and to get into trouble with. We wanted the same for our daughter.

After six months of trying and not getting pregnant, doubt set in; after all, we knew we were capable of procreating. We were young and healthy and already had a beautiful baby girl. How could there possibly be a problem?

The doctor informed us that it was early in the process. Basically, we were told to relax and keep trying. Six months turned into a year. I began to wonder if I would ever get pregnant again.

Time marched on. Our closest friends and family members knew our desire to have another baby. We watched as some of them announced their pregnancies and future deliveries. Celebrating with each of them, but we longed to do the same. What was taking God so long? Were we being punished?

One year turned into two years. Then, one evening, while attending a prayer meeting at church, a dear friend came up to me and whispered in my ear, "God has not forgotten you. As an act of faith, I want you to buy a jar of baby food and a pacifier and write your baby's name on it. Leave the items out in the open so you can see them every day."

We did as she suggested. We even got our daughter involved. It would be a great lesson of faith for all of us. We stood on Scripture, *"(As it is written, I have made thee a father of many nations,) before him whom he believed, even God, who quickeneth the dead, and calleth those things which be not as though they were."* **Romans 4:17 KJV.** We purchased a crib and converted the home office into a nursery. The nursery door remained open, and we called out to Michael whenever we passed by.

Time marched on. Two years turned into two and a half years. Month after month, we purchased at-home pregnancy tests, each one announcing the disappointment. Friends and family members continued to announce their pregnancies and deliveries. Even friends who didn't want to be pregnant were having babies. When I could no longer take the disappointment, I told my husband I no longer wanted to spend money on pregnancy tests. But we continued to speak words of faith in our home.

Time marched on. Two and a half years turned into three years. On Mother's Day 1994, while sitting in church service, I heard a still small voice tell me to buy a pregnancy test. I did like Mary in **Luke 2:19**. I kept it to myself and pondered it in my heart. After church, I asked my husband to stop by the store so I could run in to get something. He agreed. I ran into the store while he stayed in the car with Ashley. Making sure the test kit was well disguised among the other purchases in my bag, I returned to the car without letting them in on my secret.

When we arrived at home, I headed straight for the bathroom. After what seemed like eons, a clear blue line appeared on the strip. I was pregnant! I couldn't wait to share the news with my husband and daughter. Both were overjoyed. We praised God right then and there. It was a joyous Mother's Day.

Eight months later, we welcomed our son, Michael, to the family.

This is my testimony. Perhaps you have had a similar experience. I urge you to lean and depend on God. As children of God, we can be assured He is in control. Don't give up. Keep praying and believing. If you have been called according to his purpose, things will work out for your good.
Romans 8:28 KJV

About Waletta

W. Mason Dunn is an accomplished best-selling author and writing consultant who is passionate about spreading the good news of the Gospel through her writing. Waletta uses her gift of writing to give testimony to God's love for us. She has written and published six novels, and many more are in the works.

Born in Bossier City, Louisiana, Waletta was raised in a loving Christian home, learning the values and virtues that shape one to live in the likeness of Christ. A firm believer in continuous learning and self-improvement, she pursued and earned an undergraduate degree in Business Administration from Texas College and a graduate degree in Public Administration from the University of Oklahoma.

A highly motivated and dedicated professional, Waletta worked for more than two decades in higher education as a counselor for the military while traveling with her husband before he retired from the United States Marine Corps after 20 years of distinguished service. Her personal and professional experiences heavily influenced and contributed to her literary works, inspiring her to document what God has done for her through the good, bad, and ugly times.

Waletta is a committed wife who has been married to her loving husband for close to four decades. They are the parents of two young adult children, Michael Stewart. When she is not busy working on her next literary project, Waletta enjoys reading, playing Scrabble, solving crossword puzzles, and helping others.

Amazing Grace
DORIAN EVANS

My name is Dorian Evans, and I am a sinner who has been saved by God's amazing grace. Whenever I fall short of all that God had designed me to be, he is there to pick me up, dust me off, and put me back together. As I grow closer to Christ in my walk, I realize that I don't fall as much or as fast as I did from the last time I fell. I often beat myself up more than my father in heaven does. The Bible says, "For though the righteous fall seven times, they rise again, but the wicked stumble when calamity strikes."**Proverbs 24:16 NIV**

This particular time was a lot different than when I had fallen before. This time, I have been in this waiting season for what feels like forever. Waiting for prayers to be answered takes patience, faith, and trust. One area of our life can often grow when trusting God, while another can be lacking without us realizing it.

I often feel so alone in this world. I am trying to be like the example God has given us, and I mean *really* trying. I remember asking God, "Why? Why do I feel so alone? I'm not as strong as Jesus." I remember hearing him say, "Jesus was never alone; he was always surrounded by his 12 disciples, and the one time he was alone, he was tempted." I replied, "Yes, but he did not fall."

At that moment, I still did not know what the answer was. I repented immediately and continued to get ready for church. I arrived at church and took a seat. I sat in the sanctuary and felt guilty for letting God down, even though I knew I had been forgiven. Again, feeling alone and unloved, and questioning, "Why am I trying to live this life of the believer when it feels so isolating?" Did you know they don't call it loneliness anymore; they call it solitude as if that makes it less painful?

God has a way of meeting you right where you are, and that's what He did; His love met me right there, removed the void I was filling, and slowly started replacing it with His love and peace while covering me yet again with His *amazing grace*. The following Sunday confirmed what my dear friend Jackie had said to me just the night before. My pastor spoke out of the book of Ephesians.

Again, the word of God met me right where I was and answered the very question of why I am living the life I was living in verses 17-18. "So I tell you this, and insist on it in the Lord, that you must no longer live as the Gentiles do, in the futility of their thinking. They are darkened in their understanding and separated from God's life because of their ignorance and the hardening of their hearts." ***Ephesians 4:17-18 NIV***

I learned two things during this season of life.

First, God's grace is sufficient, and while I do not know why my waiting season is so long for some of the things I have prayed for, I do know God has not forgotten about me; He loves me, and while I am walking this walk, I cannot do it alone. I must reach out when the solitude is too much, reaching out to like-minded individuals will encourage me to stay on my path. Stop thinking you are a burden! I am sure you have been there for someone when they needed to "phone a friend." It is ok for you to do the same.

Second, stay focused on what is going well and continue to be thankful; distractions take our focus off all God is doing in our lives. We then magnify the one area that isn't ours to deal with anyway because we have given it to God, *several times*. We make things worse when we try to reinsert ourselves or take back what we have given to Him.

If you feel alone, empty, or unloved, surround yourself with 1 to 11 other believers, submerge yourself in the word of God, and never forget that He loves you as well.

About Dorian

Dorian L. Evans is a graduate of Bowling Green State University and a mom to three sons and one daughter. Born and raised in Ohio, Evans now calls Central Texas home where she teaches high school and writes. She enjoys traveling to watch her children compete, cooking, and being with her family and friends.

Evans recently released her first two publications the book Understanding My Assignment: My journey on raising champions, trusting the process and finding who I am, and Understanding My Assignment: The planner/journal.

She has turned her vulnerabilities into strengths as she shares what she has been through in life with others in hopes it will help them through tough situations in life. Evans was raised in a single parent home and credits all of her success to her Christian upbringing, her mother, and her grandparents.

"They didn't just talk about love, they showed and continue to show it in their walk every day. All of my family is amazing, I couldn't have been born into a better family. They have shaped me into the woman and mother that I am today." Through it all she remains a strong believer and follower of Christ. "Without Him, I am nothing, in Him I can do anything!"

Faith Over Fear
SHANA GOURDINE

Once, a woman dreamt of the quintessential happy family - children, a loving husband, and a fulfilling career. But reality dealt her a different hand. Three years into a relationship, she found herself battling depression, PTSD, anxiety, and a myriad of other emotional scars. Not just one toxic relationship, but two nearly shattered her beyond repair. Blinded by youthful naivety, she endured unspeakable abuse – dragged by her hair, choked while pregnant, her very identity disrespected.

Still, she clung to the hope of a unified family, believing love meant enduring apologies and false promises of change. Until one day, clutching her infant daughter, she faced her abuser's hands around her throat. How could she continue down this dark path? Love was not meant to inflict pain.

As a small-town girl navigating the vast expanse of New York City with no familial support, her next steps were uncertain. But she knew she had to break free. Though her abuser clung to control, she refused to be a pawn in his game. There had to be more to life than this cycle of toxicity and trauma.

Yet, just as she began her journey to reclaim her life, health issues struck. Already burdened with fibromyalgia, Ankylosing Spondylitis, and Polycystic Kidney Disease, she cried out to a higher power for solace. How could she be the pillar of strength her daughters needed when she felt so broken?

Months passed in a haze of anger, frustration, and self-doubt. She questioned the fairness of her suffering, wrestling with her faith and her place in the world. But amidst the turmoil, a realization dawned – she, too, played a part in her own undoing. Seeking solace in toxic relationships and self-destructive patterns only perpetuated her pain.

Acknowledging her role in her own struggles, she embarked on a journey of self-discovery and healing. Therapy became her lifeline, a beacon guiding her back to herself. She learned that seeking help was not a sign of weakness but courage.

With each session, she reclaimed pieces of herself long lost to trauma. She forgave herself for past mistakes and found strength in vulnerability. No longer defined by her scars, she rose above her circumstances, a testament to the resilience of the human spirit.

Now, she stands as a beacon of hope, proof that there is life after trauma. She knows her worth and is secure in knowing she is loved unconditionally. No longer afraid to walk away from those who do not honor her worth, she embraces her journey with unwavering faith.

For she knows that even in the darkest of times, there is light. And though the road may be fraught with challenges, she refuses to be defeated. With each step forward, she embodies the truth that healing is possible, that strength lies within, waiting to be unleashed.

With unwavering trust, she proclaims: "God is my salvation; I will trust and not be afraid. The Lord, the Lord himself, is my strength and my defense." (Isaiah 12:2)

In the midst of my darkest moments, when despair threatened to consume me, I found an unexpected source of strength—my faith. As I embarked on the arduous journey of healing, I discovered that my walk with God would lead me to personal restoration and unveil a newfound purpose: to share my story and offer hope to others.

Guided by a divine presence, I began to unravel the tangled threads of my past, confronting the demons that had long haunted me. With each step, I found solace in prayer, drawing courage from believing I was not alone in my struggles.

As I delved deeper into my faith, I realized that my scars were not merely symbols of pain but testaments to resilience. They were reminders of the battles I had fought and the victories I had won. With each scar, I discovered a story waiting to be told - a story of redemption, of triumph over adversity.

Embracing my newfound purpose, I embarked on a journey of self-discovery and self-expression. Through writing, I found a voice to articulate the complexities of my journey, to weave together the fragments of my shattered past into a tapestry of hope.

But I sought more than just my own healing. Inspired by the transformative power of my own story, I made a solemn vow to use my experiences to uplift others. I became determined to turn my pain into purpose, to offer a guiding light to those who walked the same dark path I once traversed.

And so, armed with pen and paper, I set out to share my testimony with the world. With each word penned, I poured out my heart, baring my soul to those who dared to listen. Through the pages of my books, I offered a glimpse into the depths of my struggles and the heights of my triumphs.

But more than mere words on a page, my books became beacons of hope, guiding others through their own journey of healing and self-discovery. They became empowerment tools, inspiring readers to embrace their scars as badges of honor and to find strength in their vulnerability.

As I witnessed the impact of my words on the lives of others, I knew that I had found my calling. I had become not just an author but a messenger of hope, a beacon of light in a world shrouded in darkness.

So, I continue to walk this path with God by my side, allowing my testimony to illuminate the way for others. With each book I write, I reaffirm my commitment to healing—both for myself and for those who journey alongside me.

I have learned that our scars are not meant to be hidden away in shame but to be proudly worn as symbols of our strength and resilience. In sharing our scars with the world, we find healing not just for ourselves but for all who are touched by our stories.

About Shana

Shana was born November 23,1980 in Charleston, SC. She was raised in Cross, SC by her mother Viola Gourdine and Great-Grandmother Jaine B. Smalls. She graduated high school from Cross High school in Cross, SC on June 1999. Shana graduated from Morris College in Sumter, SC in May 2003 with a BA in Sociology. She obtained her culinary arts certificate in 2015 from ACAP.

Shana is the mother of two beautiful girls, Leonna Gourdine-Walker and Samira Gourdine-Walker who she loves dearly. They are her heart and soul. She moved to Troy, New York in June 2003 to pursue her career. Shana entered into the work force as a produce clerk and cashier to start her journey.

In 2004, Shana was blessed with a job at the Center For

Disability Services. She served as a Residential Counselor and an Assistant Manager for four years. She served many different companies over the years until she found out she has three different conditions that set limits to her work journey. Shana battles fibromyalgia, Ankylosing Spondylitis, polycystic kidney disease, and polycystic ovary syndrome. Now, she has entered a new journey as an Author of , "The Mask Behind the Mask", a motivational speaker, the CEO of Shana Unmasking Motivation, and the owner of G&G Jewelry. In addition, Shana is a part of PWG, HTM Organization, and an Advocate for Domestic Violence. Shana was awarded the 2019 Purple Ribbon Award of Courage.

A Breakdown to Breakthrough
NATASHIA HAGANS

I'll be as transparent as I can be as I share my journey with you. The best advice I can give is to take care of your mental health before it takes care of you! In 2016, I ignored the red flags, and I didn't slow down to process the trauma that I had to deal with that year. My year began with my mom being robbed at gunpoint; both of my grandmothers died six months apart; my father was diagnosed with cancer, and work and home lives were stressful. While all this occurred, I was in grad school working on completing a twenty-page paper for final exams.

I felt the physical effects of all of these stressors: my back started tingling, and I tried to go to sleep after three days. I ended up in the emergency room in a panic. The result of the emergency room visit was an evaluation to the psychiatric ward and a sleeping pill prescription called Ambien. I went on with my life like it was nothing.

Still, the side effects of being on these sleeping pills were mood swings, suicidal thoughts, severe depression, loss of appetite, irritable bowel syndrome, and hair loss. I went to the doctor for a follow-up, and she told me I can't let you have these sleeping pills anymore. I became frantic and in a panic as I got blood work done.

My doctor called me in immediately and told me I had harmful bacteria in my stomach. I was sent to a gastroenterologist, where I got a colonoscopy at age 35, and this is when they found a benign tumor in my intestine. I was also referred to a psychiatrist, who I could tell was burned out and wasn't a good fit for me. I was experimenting with pills that were not working for me due to the side effects like wanting to die, drinking bleach, and banging my head against the wall. I told myself, "This is enough." I confided in a few people, and they told me, "Tashia, this is not you!" "Get yourself checked out." I decided to get myself checked out. I had a conversation with my primary care doctor, and I felt I needed to be checked back into the psychiatric ward in 2017.

Once I checked in to the psychiatric ward, I told it all. I could barely speak and was stuttering badly. I was taken off of the medications for my mental health. I stayed in the mental ward for a week. I didn't forget the earth angels that were sent to me during my breakdown. I was diagnosed with major depressive disorder and a high pulse rate due to anxiety and placed on the proper medication.

I was out of the mental hospital in a cold, dark room. The nurse told me, "You don't belong here." After being placed on the correct medication, I started to slowly come back to myself. When people started seeing me drift, they would tell me to snap out of it. But I remember God so vividly whispering in my ear, "I have more work for you to do!"

My mother picked me up from the hospital and took me to get clothes and a journal. I was on FMLA from work for two months and just started writing, and it was a sense of relief as I journaled my thoughts. I found writing to be a gift. Writing turned my breakdown into a breakthrough. I turned that journal into a book in 2020. As I went through this journey, I found that my breakdown was a testimony to my breakthrough.

About Natasha

Natashia Evette Hagans was born at Portsmouth Naval Hospital in Virginia on August 13, 1978. She grew up in Washington, DC, and Landover, MD. Natashia has a bachelor's degree in early childhood education and is currently teaching.

Natashia's passion is writing to inspire herself and others. She has collectively written and engaged in speaking events with several heartfelt poems. Many of Natashia's poems have been showcased in newsletters, digital magazines, and anthologies.

Additionally, she is a published author who published a book on March 25, 2020, titled "Rebirth: Unfolding of the Mind through Poetry," a collection of poems about releasing thoughts. Other books Natashia published include "I Am A Butterfly," "Uncaged Butterfly," poetry books, and "Pretty Wings" for survivors of domestic violence.

Natashia continues to write her creative thoughts to be added to many more anthologies and books.

Wait, It's God's Plan
MELANIE JOHNSON

"Confess your faults to one another, and pray one for another, that ye may be healed.

The effectual fervent prayer of a righteous man availeth much." ~ **James 5:16 KJV**

I used to be afraid to speak about my issues. I felt that so many people were in worse conditions than I was, so it wasn't fair for me to dump my problems onto them. Yes, I was in an abusive marriage, but some people were in more violent situations than me (*my husband mentally and financially abused me for 23 years*). I did not wear my abuse on my face, so people would not believe me if I did try to share. This was my daily conference with myself, thinking I had to suffer alone.

But that was not true. As much as I tried to believe that I was hiding the abuse, when I finally reached out to some people in my circle, after much prayer, I was amazed at what I heard. They had seen the abusive ways and wondered how I was able to stay. Oh my. If I had only trusted God more and reached out for help when I needed it, I could have found peace in my life a lot earlier. But it was my fear of being "embarrassed" that held me back.

When God is in your life, and you are in His Will, He will protect you from all destruction. Many believe that He won't let you suffer at all. But that is not true. Your suffering will NOT be in vain. He will protect you in your suffering, but His Will is for you to emerge victorious. You WILL WIN.

Nevertheless, it will be in His timing, not yours. You must go to God expecting (believing) deliverance, but you can't give Him a timeline for when it gets done. His day is like a thousand years, so time is of no essence with Him. Just keep believing, trusting that He will make a way. And when He does, you will not be able to number (count) the blessings bestowed upon you. I know from experience. That is why you are reading these words today. Be blessed and be patient. God isn't finished yet.

Life has its share of good times and bad,

Some of the best and worst times you've ever had.

Sometimes, it's as if you'll never get a break.

Hold on, don't give up

No matter what it takes. You see

God did not create us to suffer alone

But we don't like to ask for help, as if that's something wrong.

No, just like we celebrate together our joys and praise,

We should unite on our sister's or brother's behalf

With heads bowed and hands raised

Yes, God hears the plight of the suffering man

But the unity is for us, so we can feel less pressure with the helping hand.

Yet you can't tell your woes to just anybody, that's clear.

No, ask God for discernment on who needs to share your

Good, bad, ugly and in between

Wait for His direction, for He knows what is not foreseen.

And when you pray for a healing, be careful what you say

Your words have a way to display what your heart will convey.

You must pray, believing that it will come to pass

Fervently, passionately, trusting the Father is how you should ask.

If your heart isn't in it, it is just calling words

God is faithful to each of us, so let your love for Him be heard

In your daily talk, not rehearsed rhetoric to sound good.

Take your cares to Him and leave them there

His handling of the situation should be understood.

But don't get discouraged in your long-suffering and wait.

God has a plan for you, and it will come to pass…

You just don't know the time or the date.

~ © 2024 Melanie M Johnson

About Melanie

The third of four children, **Melanie M. Johnson** grew up in rural Carthage, Mississippi to Dr. Curtis and Merl Johnson. Melanie embraced her creativity and began sewing at age 12. She loved to create crafts and unique apparel. This love for creativity would serve her well as she explored her opportunities as she grew older. Graduating as valedictorian of her high school class was quite an accomplishment, but what would lie ahead in Melanie's life was just as remarkable.

As a survivor of domestic abuse, Melanie walked away from her 23-year marriage with nothing more than her dignity and the support of her family and friends. She used the trauma she endured to begin to journal, which turned into her first publication, *Womanly Wisdom: What "they" Couldn't Tell Me*, an account of how she learned to love and respect herself despite how others treated her. This 5-star publication propelled Melanie on the scene as a motivational speaker and domestic abuse advocate, allowing her to use her words to become "The Voice" for those who couldn't speak. She has used her platform to create her own publishing company, publish her poetry book, *Flavor of Melanin*, and participate in several anthologies.

Social media links can be found here ~ https://www.linktr.ee/MelanieJohnson

Forgiving Without An Apology
PAMELA NANCE JOHNSON

Most of us, as children, were taught to say "I'm sorry" or apologize when we've hurt someone's feelings or maybe even taken something that didn't belong to us. Sometimes, the apology came quickly to avoid punishment or grudgingly when forced by the adult in charge. In any case, it was understood that the offended party would forgive and forget whatever had taken place. To move on like it never happened. I have even heard the Bible being used in reference here over the years. After much research and consultation with trusted sources, there is no confirmation to prove it.

I'd rather not focus as much on the forgetting but on the act of forgiving itself. Most times, we expect a sincere apology to come first. However, that means the guilty person must admit to their wrong. They must own it, take responsibility, and humbly ask for our compassion and understanding. What happens when you don't get an apology? Do you still forgive?

We find a very important reason to forgive others in Mark 11:24, "Therefore I tell you, whatever you ask for in prayer, believe that you have received it, and it will be yours. 25 And when you stand praying, if you hold anything against anyone, forgive them, so that your Father in heaven may forgive you your sins." (New International Version)

What about when you are in an abusive relationship or toxic environment? What about when you have a tragic experience, and the guilty person never comes through with a confession? What then? How long do you wait before you start to heal and move on? What do you do in the meantime? For me, prayer has been the key. Yes, even with the anguish of a broken heart, I've had to ask God to soften my heart so I could move on. At one of the most difficult times in my life, I heard the song "A Heart That Forgives" by Kevin Levar, in which one verse is:

Cause the heart that forgives is the heart that will live

Totally free from the pain of the past

And the heart that let's go

It is the heart that will know so much freedom.

Unforgiveness can also affect our physical health. The negative health effects can include stress, increased depression, anxiety, and social isolation. You can worry yourself sick and the other person will have gone on about their business. Meanwhile, you are aching and suffering because of holding in your feelings. Depending on the situation, you may need to seek mental health counseling from a professional. Protecting your peace is vital to your spiritual, mental, and physical health.

Even more than the apology, I wanted to be free and at peace. It wasn't easy and didn't come quickly, but when I forgave my transgressor, I felt like the biggest weight had been lifted from me. The burden I had carried just holding on to the hurt was no longer there. That feeling I'd get just reliving certain moments had gone. It no longer matters whether I hear those words. I honestly pray that the person can ask God to forgive them before it's too late. Guilt, anger, and regret are not things that we should take to the grave.

Recently, I was asked if I hold grudges and, if not, how is that possible. Do I harbor unforgiveness? I took a moment to explain that I would have answered yes in the past. I gave a couple of my go-to scriptures when those feelings come up, as they will. As for matters of the heart, I look to Psalm 51:10: "Create in me a clean heart, O God; and renew a right spirit within me." I start each day as new, remembering Lamentations 3:22. Because of the Lord's great love, we are not consumed, for his compassions never fail. 23 They are new every morning; great is your faithfulness."

Forgiving itself can be hard; without a sincere apology, it is even harder. However, when we ask God to help us, our hearts can heal, and we will find peace and guidance to move on with our lives. When released from the burden, we have the freedom to live, thrive, and be all we are called to be. We can use our gifts for God's glory while encouraging others. When I allowed myself to be vulnerable and start writing, I understood more that God has been building my testimony. He has given me the strength to share with others, especially women. I pray that you will be inspired by our shared stories. If I can make a difference in one person's life, then I believe God is well pleased.

About Pamela

Pamela Nance Johnson is a lover of Christ, an author, a minister, and an entrepreneur. Pamela enjoys sharing the gospel of Jesus Christ with those she encounters daily. She also loves lifting praise to our Lord and Savior through song. Follow Pamela on Facebook @PamelaNanceJohnson and email at pamelanjohnson@gmail.com

A Love Letter From Your First Love
CHARISE KING

I am writing this letter to you because I have seen the struggles that you have gone through. The thoughts that have pondered your mind, I understand the world has been rough on you...Childhood trauma, Social media, life circumstances and situations, and relationships that you hoped to be promising. I have never left you; I have been here all along. Did you hear the small whisper of, I love you? When I stopped the relationships you wanted to continue, it was me saying I Love you. I want you to know that I have watched and been there with you every step.

This is a love letter to tell you how proud I am of you. You made it through all the obstacles that have presented themselves to you. You believed with blind faith, no matter what others thought of you. I know that it was hard to do. Here are the things I thought of you when I formed and knitted you in the deepest, darkest places. Remember, I knew you before I formed you in your mother's womb. Jeremiah1:5

I have good plans for you, not harm but hope and a future. Jeremiah 29-11.

My heart knows that you have a purpose, I have plans for you, and I have a promise. To whom much is given, much is required. Luke 12:48

I will hold no good thing from you. Psalm 84:11 You are equipped and covered to my promises for you. You are the dream, the curse breaker. I am your heavy load bearer. I thought of you while you were just a mist. I smiled, I was overjoyed, and I fell in love with you. So, whenever you feel that you have no one to love or are not enough, remember what I have said. I have loved you from the very beginning. You will have other loves that no one can compare to mine. The love that I have shown you will teach you to love yourself so that you will only accept a love that will pray for you, protect you, plan with you, and provide in a way that comes from me. Your First Love... It's time to forgive, live, and love yourself completely as I have loved you.

Signed,

Your True Love

A=Apple of my eye, Anointed, Appointed, and Adored

B Bold, Brilliant, Brains and Beautiful

C=Caring, Compassionate, Courageous, and Confident

D=Direct, Dedicated, Determined, and Discipline

E=Excellence, Educated, Elegance and Extraordinary

G=Glamorous, Gorgeous, Go-Getter and Grateful

H=Happy, Humorous and Hopeful

I= Intelligence, Intellect, and Informative

J= Joyous

K= Kind, Kings Child, and Knowledgeable

L= Love, Luxurious, Laughter Luminary

M=Motivated, Mindful, and Manner

N=Noteworthy, No Sense

O=Optimistic

P=Peculiar, Pretty, Persistent, and Patience

Q=Quick

R=Ready, Realistic, and Rewarding

S=Steady, Stable, Stupendous

T=Talent, Tactful

U=Unusual, Unique

V=Valuable, Valid

W=Wisdom, Worthy, and Wife

X=Xenial, Xenas

Z=Zeal, Zest

These are the many things that describe you throughout your life. I am your first Love before you were ever a thought. Anything else is contrary to what I have said. Focus and think on these things.

Love Letters from Your First True Love

About Charise

Charise King is a multi-talented individual, known for her dynamic roles as CEO of "What She Said" Productions, Speaker, Emcee, Host, Voice-Over Actor, and now, an Actor. With a remarkable career, Charise has made her mark in various domains.

Under the banner of "What She Said" Productions, Charise has curated captivating experiences through her speaking engagements, emceeing, hosting, and voice-over work. Her versatility is evident as she seamlessly transitions from one role to another.

Adding to her accomplishments, Charise is the creative force behind the "Chattin' and Chillin' with Lady Charise" Facebook page, and she maintains a strong presence on "What She Said" Productions' LinkedIn page and @chattinwcharise on TikTok.

As a host, Charise has orchestrated remarkable events such as the Tina Marie Girl's Day Party and Champagne Brunch, as well as the Maricopa Indoor Block Party. Her involvement in the Motivational Speakers Forum, fondly known as "Powerhouse," showcases her dedication to inspiring and uplifting others.

Charise's influence extends further as a Member of the Black of Commerce, NAREB National Association of Real Estate Brokers Local Phoenix Chapter, and Arizona Small Business Association a testament to her commitment to fostering connections and community.

In January 2022, Charise attained her Voice Coach certification, solidifying her prowess as a voice actor. Her journey can be explored further at www.whatshesaid.biz, where you can book her services and explore the events she has skillfully hosted.

The Call
GWYN MAIS

I spent hours and hours that day waiting for the call that would radically change my life.

Waiting is not easy! All I could think about was him and how broken he must feel, which broke my heart even more. A very close family member had taken seventy-one Tylenol and didn't tell anyone for three days. My heart couldn't really distinguish what to feel. It had too many feelings raging at the same time to understand what they all were.

Although the rest of my world was foggy and tuned out, my ears waited to hear the phone ring. With that one ring, I knew I would know if he was still in this world with us. On the other end of the phone, I heard that he had a 50/50 shot of being here with us tomorrow. The night would be touch and go. My heart sank knowing that for the rest of the night, I had to live with this state of complex feelings raging that spilled over in a puddle of tears mixed with a lot of fear.

I was waiting, but I had no idea that my waiting period had only just begun and that this nightmare was only the beginning of a string of nightmares. While he made it through the night and the Lord blessed him with a miraculous recovery, my heart was damaged. I had no idea how damaged I was until I began to carry more and more trauma in the years to come.

After this family tragedy, it seemed we were supposed to be grateful the Lord healed him and move on. While I was grateful for that, I couldn't move on. I didn't know how to move forward but didn't know how to heal. So, I was stuck. I was in limbo between not wanting to move on with my life because it felt wrong to do so and not seeing any other way but to sweep it all under the rug and keep trucking along so that God wouldn't think we were ungrateful.

These ideas formed partially from my own emotional turmoil, lack of experience with this kind of pain, and the enemy coming in, forming lies inside my head that I accepted somewhat unknowingly. I had no idea the full extent of the complexities going on inside me until years later.

Over the next fourteen years, my heart grew heavier, and that rug no longer seemed to hide all that was swept under it. I was more than stuck in a cycle, I was drowning in life. I walked through two miscarriages. I had a husband with a pornography addiction and calling a woman to his room, a pregnancy that wasn't supposed to be viable, sexual assault while my husband was deployed, and losing several friends to suicide... and that was just the highlight.

That last one broke me. I couldn't carry anymore. Waiting for the season to end was over; I had instead waited for more pain to come; I knew it was around the corner. This mindset of waiting for the pain to come seemed so normal to me that I thought God had just decided I was able to take it all, and this was just part of life, and the pain was just a part of who I was.

It was a deep lie that the enemy fed me for years. I didn't realize anything was different until I was so broken I just let it all go to Him. I collapsed in his arms the day I found out my friend, my good friend, took her life at the tender age of 23. I came to Him on my knees and told Him it was too much, that I couldn't pick up all the pieces of my heart.

He gently responded with, "Who asked you to do that? It's my job." That forever changed my life and the trajectory of where I was headed. Through a rapid healing process, I realized how to begin to give things to God and work through the hardships in life in a healthy way. It was during that process that God called me to coach. I wasn't done with those hardships, though.

It was a few years later, in three weeks, that I found myself on my knees again in front of the Lord after losing my job, having issues with my vision, losing all of our possessions in a move (everything literally gone), and my husband asking for a divorce and confessing to an affair. On my knees this time, I found myself, arms raised in the air, praising Him for showing me how to walk through this season.

I not only knew that I could walk through hard things in a healthy and real way, but I also knew if I could praise Him through this and still be real and raw with how I felt, others could too. That which God asked me to teach worked so well that I could walk through such a storm praising Him amid my pain. I was forever changed by the waiting room I stood in for 14 years.

The Lord knew how to interweave that waiting into good for many reasons in my life but also good for others' lives as well. My marriage is still together today and thriving in a way I didn't ever think possible. I now help women across the globe with their marriages and how to heal and reconcile after pornography addictions, infidelity, or deep betrayals. He used the pain for a purpose!

You, my friend, are no different! Your pain can have a vital purpose in your life! Don't lose hope in the tragedies and traumas of this life. Fall into the Father's arms and let Him do the heavy lifting! All you need to do is be still in the waiting.

About Gwyn

Gwyn Mais is a wife of 18 years, mother of two girls, Christian life coach, veteran, and most of all child of God! Her experiences with trauma and hardships in life have shaped her heart for those going through really difficult things inside of their marriage.

She helps couples around the globe to reconcile their marriages after pornography addictions, infidelity, or deep betrayals. God gave her a massive heart to heal people's marriages from the inside out using His principles and incorporating the Holy Spirit into the entire process.

Gwyn is living proof that God can use ALL things for the good of those who love Him!

The Waiting Room For Acceptance
ALLAINA MARIA

"While I was in the waiting room for acceptance, I am so glad God was always there."

There is a time to live and a time to die. The Bible speaks to that fact. As a believer, I hold the good book and the contents therein as a life guide. However, the truth doesn't change the reality of living without the one you love. In December 2007, I gave birth to a micro preemie, born 1 pd, 6oz. He was my miracle child who lived 6 months. He brought me so much joy in his short life. He passed away in June of 2008. I never had the chance to bring him home from the hospital. He lived in the NICU his entire short life. I'll never forget that phone call that he was not having a good day and I should get to the hospital. I loaded up my car and headed over.

I walked into his hospital room and saw my son struggling to breathe. We locked eyes, and I saw the distress in his tiny face. I placed my bags on the chair adjacent to his crib and hurriedly went by his side. I held his hand and kissed his fat cheeks. Moments later, the machines began to scream. Dings, bells, and alarms rang loudly, alerting the staff that my sweet baby needed assistance. Doctors and nurses ran in from every direction, attempting to resuscitate my son. I watched helplessly with bated breath as they pumped his little chest. The look of defeat and tear-stained eyes filled the room once the reality set in that my son was gone. His tiny body had no more strength to fight. He waited for his mommy to get there to say goodbye.

Life after that was excruciating. It hurt for me to take the slightest breath. I recall lying on my living room floor in a disheveled heap, unable to lift my head for days on end. The weight of his absence felt as if an anvil sat in my chest, pinning me to the floor. I had no more tears to release. My soul was all cried out, but my spirit wept inside me.

I have always been a woman of faith, but this tested my faith beyond the brink. I was so distraught that my grief was grieving. I needed a way to get God's attention, to show him how I was hurting. I felt so abandoned and mistreated by the God I served. I recall a moment when I took invisible arrows and shot them toward the sky at God, hoping to hit him in the heart. Yes, it made no sense, but my sense and sensibility were out the window then. I wanted God to feel my pain.

One day, the new pastor of my old church and two members stopped by my apartment. He had heard about me and that I was a singer and past member of the church. He sat and chatted for a while, lifting my spirits with his sincerest condolences for my loss coupled with an earnest prayer on my behalf. The pastor also extended an invitation for me to come to church.

I struggled to think about church, let alone step foot in one. I was a broken-hearted girl who felt deserted by the one she served. I have always sung in church and led songs, but I had no song to sing. There was no joy in my vocal cords, no music in the air above my head. But what was there was a dark cloud—a veil of sadness and ashes.

Over time, the notion that a pastor would come knock on my door out of concern for my well-being put a stitch in my broken heart that I deemed irreparable. But it actually felt good to know that stranger was concerned about me. I realized that I hadn't been forgotten. Someone cared. Eventually, I took up the offer to visit the church. Shortly thereafter, I started singing on the praise team and in the choir again.

Honestly, some moments felt so awkward lifting my hands in worship because, truthfully, I still felt so hurt and betrayed by God for my son's death. However, the more I came, the better I began to feel. I truly understood the Bible regarding a time for everything, even death. It was my time to experience loss. Yes, I still hurt, but I also got to a place where I realized my son's death was not a punishment to me. It never was. It was a part of life that we all must face one day. Acceptance began to bloom in my heart. My son's journey wasn't long, but it was his journey. I had to understand that his time on earth was his time. As bad as I wanted him to stay, I could not reverse it.

The very one I was angry with, 'God,' was the one who helped me be ok. God did that for me by using the gifts he instilled in me. Even when I refused to pray or acknowledge him in my early stages of grief, he never stopped loving me. God held me through my humanity with His eternal arms. He understands the hurt. He was there when he gave His son for our right to live eternally with Him. His love for me goes from everlasting to everlasting. God's strength was made perfect in my weakest moment.

About Allaina

Allaina Maria lives her life out loud and intentionally. She is a singer, songwriter, motivational speaker, author, screenwriter and entrepreneur. Allaina passionately writes music that soothes the ears and calms the soul. She sings lead vocals on the Album, "Songs of the Lord".

Allaina's pen is unmatched as she skillfully writes Fiction, Urban Fiction, Poetry, Science Fiction, Self-help, Romance, and Children's Books, dubbing her a '360 Author'." "Mariah" released in 2023, is her debut novel and will also serve as her debut as a screenwriter.

Allaina is a first-rate motivational speaker. Her powerful words of insight encourage, fortifies, and builds up the listener. In addition, Allaina is gearing up to soon release her candle and T-shirt brand.

Allaina is the youngest of 3 girls. She is a native of Daytona Beach, Florida. She is the mother of two beautiful daughters who fuel her everyday life.

In The Eyes of the Beholder
DR. AUDREYANN MOSES

I have often wondered what it means when we say, "In the eyes of the beholder." Whose eyes are doing the beholding? I often wondered which was more important, someone beholding me or me beholding them. And where does the "beholding myself" come into play?

For those who might not be sure of the definition of "beholding," it means to "look favorably upon or to gaze upon." Now Jesus says we should "Love our neighbor as ourselves... (Matthew 22:39). So this means we would have to behold ourselves favorably – meaning we must first love ourselves. Otherwise, how can we possibly love someone else?

We have often found ourselves saying or have heard others say, "I wish I looked like her/him." "Does this shirt make me look too thin, too fat, or too ugly?" "Why can't I sing, dance, paint like them?" "I hate my (fill in the blanks)." And yes, boys and men do have the same issues. Remember what it was like to look in the mirror and dislike what you saw. I remember criticizing my fat bowlegs, my features, or my hair, trying to see, to no avail, what others saw when they said I was "cute." I did not know anything about the psychological implications of self-image. Although I knew about being made in God's image, it did not help me understand I was continually lowering my own ability to love myself by being so critical of myself.

I remember someone telling me they noticed it was hard for me to accept a compliment. They were right when I thought about it because I did not see the qualities others saw in me. Since then, with much coaching, I've come to see just how much of an obstacle self-criticism can be. If teenagers do not learn to appreciate their bodies, abilities, and accomplishments, they are likely to develop issues of self-criticism into adulthood. God says He created us in His own image. (Genesis 1:27) Most of us believe God is beautiful, kind, and loving, and He loves us unconditionally. However, we don't use it to see beauty in ourselves. We spend a lot of money trying to remake ourselves into our image - what we think we should look or be like. For instance - a woman who cannot accept God's creative blueprint for her body will have difficulty accepting the honest love and admiration of the man God sent for her. If he tells her she is beautiful, she will assume he's lying or blind. If a man does not have faith in his own accomplishments and abilities, why should he believe it when friends and family tell him he is a great husband, dad, deacon, piano player, auto mechanic, etc.

People (men and women) who are self-deprecating are rarely able to receive the gift of a sincere compliment, the honest love of others, and the unconditional love of God. We constantly limit relationships with others because we worry about how others see us. Because we behold ourselves so critically and harshly, we cannot rationalize how someone else can see our beauty, not even God. We don't realize we are providing ammunition for others to treat us as inadequate and unattractive. Basically, they are treating us the way we treat ourselves.

When we were created – on the day we were born AND every day we wake up, God says, "She is good – He is good" (Genesis 1:31). If we allow God to live in our spirits, we will begin to see more good and beauty in ourselves. Ask your spouse, children, boss, and friend what they see in you? You will be surprised to know they love you just because you are you, because you are a kind, generous, and talented person. Most of all, they love you because you are BEAUTIFUL – inside and out. I tried it, and it worked wonders for my self-image.

As we begin this new day, remember to BEHOLD YOURSELF and see the image of God – "Having the Glory of God: and her light was like unto a stone most precious, even like a jasper stone, clear as crystal." (Revelation 21:11). YOU are that Precious Stone.

About Dr. AudreyAnn

My name is **Dr. AudreyAnn Moses**, and I would first like to thank you for allowing the inspiring words of "The Women of the Waiting Room: Surgery for Your Soul – Devotional." to provide added inspiration to your day. I am a Certified Christian Life Coach, Speaker, Workshop Facilitator, and award-winning, bestselling Author. I am also a United States Navy Chief Petty Officer (Retired), wife, mother, grandmother, and great-grandmother.

I love talking to people, and I especially love helping people see God in all of their life's plans. Please browse my website to learn more about me, my philosophy and practice as a Life Coach, and my books (https://www.transitionlifecoach4u.com).

I pray that God will continue to shower you with His love and blessings, and you will use those blessings to help others see how much He loves them.

No Weapon
KIMBERLY PARKS

"No weapon formed against you shall prosper, and every tongue which rises against you in judgment you shall condemn." (Isaiah 54:17 NKJV)

This is one of my favorite verses in the Bible. I have repeated it many times over the years for me and my family when we were going through hard times. This is the promise of God. It's dangerous for us to think that if we lead a Christian life, things will be smooth sailing and nothing harmful will come our way. This is when the enemy tries the hardest to discourage us, destroy us, and have us questioning our faith. If I didn't know that Satan was busy and at any given moment would throw everything at me but the kitchen sink, I wouldn't know how to handle the attacks. Even though Satan is busy, I have an assurance from God that his plans won't succeed.

An attack on my health was formed against me, but no sickness prospered. In December of 1996, while on our lunch break, my coworker and I were in a car accident that landed me in the hospital for a month after having to be cut out of the car by the 'jaws of life.' The accident left me with a disc pressing on a nerve and severe sciatica, which causes me to be in constant pain every day. Still, I'm blessed to have survived such a horrific accident. In January of 2014, I suffered a stroke. Little did I know that this was a wake-up call for me to make some changes in my life. A difficult marriage and a job I didn't like were the sources of my stress. I left the job and ended the marriage. I learned from those experiences that peace of mind is priceless.

I have suffered attacks on my finances. Financial insecurity and poverty did not prosper. Instead, I learned how to spend my money wisely, budget my finances better, and improve my credit score during the process.

I have suffered attacks on my character and my reputation, but slander did not prosper. I learned how to ignore that which was false and let the enemy know I would not be defeated.

I have suffered heartbreak from failed relationships, but loneliness did not prosper. I learned to work on loving myself and what made me happy. I realized I didn't have to settle for less because I know my worth.

I have suffered from anxiousness and depression, but fear did not prosper. I learned that fear was FALSE EVIDENCE APPEARING REAL.

God's word doesn't promise us a life free of problems. The truth is we will endure all kinds of issues and find ourselves at odds with other people for one reason or another, but no matter what comes our way, seen or unseen, God promises us victory.

"I can be changed by what happens to me, but I refuse to be reduced by it."-Maya Angelou

About Kimberly

Kimberly Parks is a sought-after, highly skilled, professional editor and writer with a passion for the English language and a sharp eye for details.

Kimberly's love for writing began early in elementary school where she would read everything she could get her hands on. She was probably the only one of her classmates that didn't complain when they had to write essays. She won her first essay contest in 7th grade.

Kimberly continued to excel and because she was so good at English and handwriting, some of her classmates would pay her to proofread their papers and make them legible.

Kimberly's writing and editing journey continued when she was selected to be the Editor in Chief of her high school yearbook, where she was responsible for the overall operation and publication of the yearbook. She also wrote for and became the Editor of her college newspaper.

Kimberly joined the Pa-Pro-Vi Publishing team as Editor in Chief in 2020 where she has been the editor of numerous clients publishing projects. In fact, she is the most requested. Kimberly was the editor for several #1 Best Sellers, including She Said Yes To Herself Unapologetically…The Empowerment Guide for Women by Visionary Chanelle Coleman and Mountains Can't Rise Without Earthquakes by Jacquiline Cox. Not only does Kimberly have a keen eye for detail, she also has a strong sense of editorial judgement.

Kimberly earned a Bachelor of Science in English with a Journalism Emphasis from Union College in Barbourville, Kentucky.

Kimberly has one child and lives in Atlanta. In her spare time, she enjoys freelance proofreading and copy editing for independent authors, traveling, and serving as the President for her Alumni Association.

Wrap Yourself in the Word
JONI ROSEBROCK

"I just want my wife back!" This had become my husband's desperate plea. He wanted the wife he married and raised children with—the wife before bitterness, self-hatred, and depression consumed me and smothered our joy. My usual response was to look away from his disappointment-filled eyes and do something else. I was tired of not being enough, not doing the right thing, and not acting like I used to. I was not me, and I had no idea who that person was, even if I wanted to fix it. I didn't know his wife.

"Fine, tell me who she is, and I will be her," I answered. We could end all the darkness and unhappiness if he told me who she was. I honestly thought I could just be her if he could tell me who he thought his wife was. I didn't know who I used to be. I didn't recognize who I was. I couldn't fix this.

It was hard to learn that I wasn't the fixer, nor was my husband. Work, denial, alcohol, spending, gaining more knowledge, and trying new things weren't the fixers. No one or nothing could fix it. Nothing could take away the discouragement and restore joy to my life—not my husband demanding his wife back or the monthly crate of wine on auto-delivery.

God was the only fixer, and I had to trust Him to do the fixing. Yes, something had to give, and it was me. I had to accept responsibility for my thoughts, emotions, and how I responded to the lies of my situation. I had to surrender the striving, denial, and the fact that I was not well. I had to trust that God could handle all of me and my mess.

I cried out for months and prayed this prayer daily from ***Psalm 1:3.***

"Lord, I want to be like the tree planted firmly by your living waters. Create fruit in me to grow in the seasons you had established for me before I was born. Please don't let me wither. Please fix me. I want to be alive and flourish in what You have called me to do and created me to be. Father, please let me prosper in all I do to bring Glory to You."

I was tired of being me. I was ready to surrender. God began teaching me that my deep emptiness, the longing for something more, was my desire to know more about Him. I thought I had lost God, but I hadn't. I moved away from Him, filled my life with other voices, and could not sense His presence. God never moves away from me.

I prayed repeatedly, asking God how I could be like this tree.

His answer was in verse 2 of Psalm 1.

"But they delight in the law of the LORD, meditating on it day and night."

I started studying that single verse word by word. God slowly replaced all the negative and condemning voices with His voice of love and truth as I delighted in His Word. I started by writing one verse a day.

Once He had built a loving foundation of His Truth in my heart, He led me to verse 1 of Psalm 1.

"Blessed is the man who walks not in the counsel of the wicked, nor stands in the way of sinners, nor sits in the seat of scoffers."

Was I doing what God says I should not? Was I missing His blessing carelessly walking with the wicked, sitting with sinners, and standing with scoffers? I began reading and applying His Word to my life.

I prayed as He led me in repentance like King David in **Psalm 51:10-12.**

Create in me a clean heart, O God, and renew a right spirit within me. Cast me not away from your presence, and take not your Holy Spirit from me. Restore to me the joy of your salvation, and uphold me with a willing spirit.

I continued in Psalm 51, and in the next verse, God met me with a promise I could make: He would fully honor and equip me to accomplish it.

Psalm 51:13 - Then I will teach transgressors your ways, and sinners will return to you.

As He wrapped me in His love and answered my prayers, God gifted me the practice of WRAP Yourself in the Word. He taught me to write, read, apply, and pray His Word. This personal journey led to my most significant healing. WRAP Yourself in the Word is an invitation to leave the self-centered life and live as a treasured child of God with a purpose to teach others.

What if we approached God's Word differently?

What if reading the Bible was like getting a massive hug from God?

Or sitting in your favorite comfy chair, holding a special mug filled with a warm, inviting drink?

Or snuggled in a blanket with a letter from your best friend?

Imagine longing for the next time you meet God and enjoy

His instructions.

WRAP Yourself in the Word was the answer. It showed me the fixer! And He restored my joy!

About Joni

Joni Rosebrock is married to her high school sweetheart. Celebrating four decades of marriage, they live on a grain farm in NW Ohio, where they enjoy visits from their three children and charming grandsons. She hosts a weekly podcast based on her book WRAP Yourself in the Word, A Simple Practice in Scripture that Leads to Hope and Healing.

Joni holds degrees in communications and education and a lay certification in Biblical Counseling. She loves to encourage others through coaching and speaking. She enjoys entertaining guests in her spare time at Arrowsmith Farm and Retreat, their newly restored 130-year-old brick farmhouse.

You can learn more about Joni at www.jonirosebrock.com.

My Waiting Testimony
BEVERLEY-ROSE SMITH

My name is Beverley-Rose Smith. I am a Jamaican African born and raised in St. Thomas, Jamaica.

Growing up in Jamaica during the 1970s and 1980s, I developed a deep love for the Almighty Creator from the tender age of 12. However, when I turned 15, I accepted the Lord and have been on a spiritual journey ever since.

I did not come from a church background. I did not grow up attending Sunday school or seeing my mother, Father, or grandparents worship the Almighty Creator. So, it was unknown to me what the Almighty Creator sounded like. Still, I did hear him inside of me at the age of 12, calling me to worship, with the joy and happiness of the Almighty Creator spilling over for humanity.

However, when I told my mother that I wanted to go to church to give praise and worship to the LORD, I was saddened to hear my mother telling me that I could not and what I thought I was doing. Although I did not get to attend church, it was not forgotten, but it lay deep in my spirit. When I turned 15 years old, and the opportunity presented itself, I accepted the call. It was down by the Riverside where the Church of God of Prophecy was baptizing those who had previously said yes to the Father in giving their lives to the

Lord and Saviour.

It was an incredibly happy moment for me, but that spirit was not dampened when the news reached my mother, telling her what I had done. I was determined to serve the Almighty Creator, and I became highly active in the youth group called the Victory Leading Band (VLB); low and behold, I was even accepted into the choir, although I was unaware, I had such a voice and could sing. But when I reached the age of 18 and went away on a church trip, it was at the church camp that I was filled with the holy spirit of the Almighty Creator. My relationship with the Father got deeper and closer to the point where I was witnessing to others and bringing them to the Almighty Creator; this included my own mother, who at first did not want to know.

The enemy did not like me much after all that happened, as obstacles on every side seemed to find me. I was in the fight of my young life, but I still did not know the Almighty Creator much at this point or even how he was proving himself to me. At eighteen years old, I struggled with being a teenager, wanting to do what my friends could do. I was unhappy with the church dressing that I was conformed to rather than the stylish and outlandish dress that teenagers wore, because I did not really understand.

So much was happening, and by the time I reached nineteen years old, I was married. My husband decided I had to migrate to live with him in the United Kingdom, London, in the nineties. It was there that my relationship was tested, as I had married a man who did not have the same love for the Almighty Creator and frowned upon me going to church. He had not shared his feelings before I took him as my husband, and I was too naïve to know or ask.

My relationship with the Father went up and down, back and forth for a few years, and I left the church at one point. The love of the Almighty Creator has been the primary source of my joy, peace, happiness, and forgiveness to others who have continued to hurt me throughout the years. I could not stay away for too long; I was led to go back years later because the Almighty Creator had never left my presence or side but kept his hands on me, even when I did not know it. This is because although I had escaped several terrible ordeals, I fell into several others. I realized that more dreadful things were happening when I was far away from the Father.

However, I developed a far better understanding of the Father. I communicated much better with him through prayer, fasting, singing, and dancing in worship and adoration of his love, mercy, grace, and Favor. My faith was then tested more so as I was told that I would have to leave the home I shared with my children, as it was subsiding. Although that home was shared with another tenant on the ground floor, I was on the first. I would sometimes be frightened by the tenant banging on his ceiling and the floor of my home, telling my children to stop the noise and stop playing as they were disturbing him. When asked if I would like to move to a new accommodation I accepted. Unaware, the local authority wanted to place me in a derelict Estate behind a train line.

Upon seeing the state of the place, I spoke with the Father, who removed the information they had and placed me in the exact type of home I had fasted and prayed to have, with me as the sole occupant and a garden for my children to play. The Almighty Creator had told me that the issues I had gone through were not about me. Still, I had refused to hear it, debating with the Creator, telling him it was me that had suffered, me feeling the pain and anguish felt over the years.

It became evident as I ministered, aided, encouraged, and guided others to continue to believe in the Almighty Creator.

A few years later, I received the telephone call that my beloved aunt had a heart attack and was in a coma. They had been told by doctors she did not have any brain activity and she would not make it. And her three children had decided to pull the plug within days because they said their mother would not like to live if she was going to be a vegetable. They were calling the family to tell us what had happened. Immediately after the call, the Father reminded me of the olive oil He had given me and told me to see my aunt, but first, I must go to the church I was attending to get it anointed. At first, I was puzzled when I got the olive oil from the fruit and vegetable distributor, who delivers every month but given the oil I had not asked for. I had kept it in the cupboard, I was not using olive oil at this point. I left my home in London and arrived in Leeds, led by the holy spirit to fast, pray, and anoint her in the hospital. When the children arrived on the Sunday to pull her plug, she woke up and has fully recovered. These miracles, and more I had seen through the spirit of the Father, gave me more testimonies to share with people I came across who needed the reassurance of his love for us.

About Beverely

Beverley- Rose Smith is a mother of five and one grandchild.

She is a Theologian, law graduate, an accountant and an author who writes nonfiction memoirs, fiction and self-help books. Growing up in Jamaica, Beverley-Rose experienced childhood sexual abuse, but when she migrated to the United Kingdom, she was raped and fell pregnant, which contributed to the traumas she carried into adulthood.

AUTHOR, WRITER, VISIONARY

Beverley-Rose developed a deep love for the Almighty Creator from the tender age of 12 years old, but it was only when she turned 15 years old, she accepted the Lord and has been on a spiritual journey ever since. The love of the creator has been the main source of her joy, peace happiness and forgiveness to others who have continued to hurt her throughout the years. However, this has never stopped Beverley-Rose from giving back to the community in the educational and legal charities she established.

Forgive, Grace, and Deliverance
SHARON SMITH

The Great Expectation

I've spent many tears and years trying to heal from my experience. I often wondered why this was so hard, and one day, it hit me that there was a great expectation for me to FORGET IT EVER HAPPENED...

But how? I can't unsee, unhear, un-feel, or undo my experience. There's no way possible to FORGET it. So, what does this REALLY mean? What does my healing look like as I move forward?

My father was spoiled as a kid as his mother died while he was young, forcing his older sister to raise him, all while being a child herself. So, all she knew to do was cater to his needs and give him what he wanted. No harm, no foul. She did her best.

Add insult to injury, my dad married a woman who picked up the pieces where his sister left off, coupled with the fact that I grew up in the era of "what goes on in the house stays in the house" was the evolution resolution to most situations. So not only am I expected to forget it, I am also expected to never talk about it. To some degree, my mom didn't protect me either... She protected her husband. This left me wondering what her relationship with her dad was like and why she had to seek love in the wrong place. My dad has no clue what love is or how to give it. There were no efforts to make the responsible parties responsible for what they did to me. This was definitely the era where they chose to conceal vs heal.

So here I am, dealing with generational curses and trying to forgive someone who never apologized. Again, the expectation for me to forget and pretend it never happened while struggling to heal. Childhood trauma is the worst hood to be in. It is a terrifying, dark, and dangerous place.

There is where I met depression, unhappiness, and insecurity. There is also where I came face to face with suicide. I learned to mask my emotions while wondering how to move forward by pretending that things didn't occur when I knew they did.

I kept hearing phrases like, " you better not tell nobody," "What goes on in this house stays in this house," and "Child, forget it ever happened."

Being from South Georgia was a blessing for me. Home was only an hour or so away. So, every chance I got, I went to my hometown. My cousins often thought I was just coming to visit, but in reality, I was running. I spent most of my childhood spending the night and visiting others. I was always seeking a refuge, any place but home.

The Power of Prayer

As I got older, I decided to try this prayer thing I heard so much about in church. Maybe I can FORGET! I was sent to church but never taught what or why it was necessary. My Great Aunt would always say to me, "Whatever is ailing you, chile, talk to God about it. I begin to pray, write, and tell God about my problems. I had a diary, aka journal. I wasn't sure if there was a wrong or right way to go to God, so I just did it. I was not sure if God was listening or could hear my thoughts. Sometimes, I felt that God was sick of me, but I kept trying and trusting that change was gone come, as I heard the ole folks say. For some reason, I couldn't *FORGET* the images and the smell as the events continued to play over and over in my head.

God told me to forgive, but nowhere does it say to "FORGET." WHERE DID YALL GET THAT FROM?

I had to find a way to detach, forgive, and forget so that I could begin to heal. So, first, I asked God to assure me that my mom knew I had forgiven her and that she was truly resting in peace with no regrets. Unknowingly, this was my first encounter with GRACE.

I had no clue what Grace was or how to use it, so I asked God to reveal it and its fullness.

God spoke to me and said Forgiveness and Grace are up to you. My job is to DELIVER you from the agony and pain of the experience.

You mean to tell me that all I need to do is FORGIVE someone who never apologized, offer them GRACE in consideration for their life experiences and God will DELIVER me?

I began to see it differently, pray differently, and understand that people can't give you what they don't have. I began to move forward in harmony, knowing that I was no longer bound to the bad memories of my past.

Unapologetically unhealed until I learned how to FORGIVE, GRACE, and allow God to DELIVER ME.

Game Changer

I am learning to forgive while understanding that I don't have to forget. Getting through and over it will allow healing to enter.

The Shift

The bigger shift came when my dad was diagnosed with Cancer. I had to heal my past to care for him. I had to learn to love, care for, and protect someone without resentment or restrictions who didn't do the same for me. NO ROOM FOR GRUDGES.

Lord, I need you now! I started praying and seeking God's DELIVERANCE so that I could honor my dad the way a daughter should.

Forgiveness is for you, not the other person. You don't have to forget your experience to heal from it.

Just TAP into God's promise to you.

TRANSPARENCY: Tell your truth

ACKNOWLEDGE: Accept your truth

PRAY: Tell God your truth

Your trauma, your tragedy, and your triggers do not bind you to your past. There is room for:

FORGIVENESS, GRACE AND DELIVERANCE

Disclaimer: **My dad never touched or harmed me. He just didn't protect me from those that did.**

About Sharon

ShaRon De'Nise Smith is a true Georgia Peach, born and raised in South Georgia. Instilled with down home morals and values which lead to her HUMBLE and CREATIVE SPIRIT. ShaRon began writing early in life. Her thoughts and vivid imagination ran wild during her years of journaling and poetry writing. ShaRon is a graduate of Fredrick Douglass High School and Strayer University receiving a MS. Adult Education with a concentration on Organizational Training and Development.

Currently, ShaRon is a Certified Life Coach, Registered Mediator Notary and works fulltime within the Property Management/Real Estate Industry. I promote healthy relationships and provide healthy mind set solutions to support mental wellness.

I operates with an extreme focus on positivity, betterment, and growth. We are all a work in progress.

"Faithing It...!"
SAM MARIE THOMAS

It begins with a longing, as Emily Dickinson wrote in part...the seed's wrestling, interceding, and consistencies, having dreams and desires, toiling through all manners of circumstance before we finally breakthrough, blooming where we've been planted.

I was born the last child of a two-parent household. Accustomed to being in grown folks' business, I asked my father where he was going one night as he walked about with a neat little green suitcase. "To a hotel", he says, "Is that alright?" I found no fault, so I gave him my 8-year-old permission to leave, unknowingly co-signing Daddy's departure from our home and, in essence, our lives.

My mother struggled mightily to take care of my siblings and me, never really achieving, not even a modicum of what I thought looked like success, though in hindsight, that very separation may have been her greatest victory! Within the next 10 years, I would lose my mother; my grief so great, I would pay a life-sabotaging homage to her for the next thirty-plus years!

I made a vow to myself and went about the quest to never pursue more in life than what I had seen Momma have. It was at this point, I believe that began my descent into a dark path of depression, anger, self-pity, lack of quality esteem, and a seemingly never-ending cycle of negative imaginations. Amazing! I had created my own dark narrative from the debilitating self-talk. I was actively living **Proverbs 23:7**.

But one thing I know for certain is that through all those clouds and storms, the seed still struggles to break ground getting to the other side. Faithing it, believing that anything that is birthed will struggle to survive.

I would become more and more depressed watching others reach milestones in their lives. Seeing this exacerbated my limiting thoughts and fears by reminding me I had shortcomings. I would think, "I'm too old," or "If I do it, it's not going to look right… be done right", or "Oh shoot, I thought about doing that years ago; I can't do it now because it's going to look like I copied." What a notion-as if there aren't seven billion people on the planet and five different chicken joints on every corner! There's room for it all, yet I would still sit back, be unproductive, watch others live their lives, cheer them on, and watch mine float by like the vapor James 4:14 expresses.

Interestingly, I had the distinct feeling that I was being disobedient to my life's call as a Christian. I was not living according to the plan that God had set before me. So, therein was my problem, I was trying to live according to my terms and not surrendering to my Creator. I knew I was being sifted for something greater. The thought of having to answer to God for this sabotage of His vessel was sobering to me.

One morning, as I nursed the spot on my couch like an old wound I had become a champion of, I experienced that I was being pulled inside, falling head-first down into an abyss of blackness. I woke up in a panic, praying and crying out to God! I knew something had to change. I had to take stock and evaluate my existence because I certainly was not living!

My mental state and beliefs about my personal values were a mess. Still, according to **Philippians 4:13, KJV**, I can do all things through Christ who strengthens me. However, I had to honestly believe it first! I began to realize I had an overwhelming desire to live!

I began faithing it, incorporating a regiment, a recipe for MY success! I secured counsel and started treatment to help hash out why I would fall into this quagmire of mental maladies. I chose to be more diligent about the one thing I knew to do for myself: seek God and pray.

I changed the narrative of how I viewed my life and began to write out different versions of my day if I could have it any way I saw fit. I started declaring that I would help myself by helping others! That meant I would not despise small beginnings by creating the life I wanted, even if the efforts seemed inconsequential. ***Zechariah 4:10. KJV***

Because of where I have been in my own journey, this desire for faithing it lead to the development of TRUE Legacy Life Coaching. ***James 1:27 KJV***, "Pure and undefiled religion before God the Father is this: to care for orphans and widows in their misfortune and to keep oneself unstained by the world." With TRUE Legacy, I am 'Transferring Righteousness Until Eternity.' The mission is to impact youth and young adult pregnant and parenting moms to always keep personal development and legacy building at the fore, encouraging a life of righteousness. We build legacies today for our families tomorrow, each day with each life-affirming encounter.

I've decided to keep my mother's legacy alive in other ways now. I wrote "Ice Cream for My Coffee," using her pearls of wisdom to encourage intentional living and value development for individuals and families.

My daily prayer is to let my light shine before men so they may see my good works and glorify God the Father in heaven. Matthew 5:16. Today, I am better at believing, and faithing is getting me there!

About Sam Marie

'Faithing it vs Faking it' implies that moving by true belief vs false reality is the key to success.

Sam Marie Thomas possesses a bachelor's degree in business administration, from Christian Brothers University, and an Associate's degree in public administration from Southwest Tennessee Community College both of Memphis, TN. She's certified as a life coach, and a Nurturing Parenting facilitator. Sam Marie recently released her inaugural book and journal, "Ice Cream for My Coffee".

The Enemy Tried To Steal My Identity
SHADAY VOID

God knew who you were already before you were born and in your mother's womb. In Jeremiah 1:5, God says, "Before I formed you in the womb, I knew you; before you were born, I sanctified you; and I ordained you a prophet to the nations. I'm here to share and uplift your spirits.

I was a foster child, and then I was adopted into a new family. Surrounded by generational curses, demonic spirits, and darkness, my identity was stolen from under me at a young age. I was raped and robbed of my innocence. I was introduced to sex and incest by my family at an early age. I experienced homelessness and was bouncing from house to house.

In reality, I was a victim of identity theft, using my social security number before I even had a life to get things in my own name. The enemy tried to take me out a long time ago as a child and as a young adult. Even though I didn't have the word or knowledge of scripture within me yet, music saved my life. I knew God was real because I was going through darkness after darkness and more darkness. Still, I felt like God had a shield around me to protect me from anything being thrown at me.

I was dealt a bad hand, but God made a way out of nowhere. I should not even be here after so much trauma, hurt, unanswered questions, anger, frustration, depression, and my battles with mental illness. I had to seek after God for healing and peace. God spiritually gave me my identity back. I know who I am: a child of God. The enemy took my identity through things and man. But God restored me and blocked the counterfeit from the enemy. I am the original, not a duplicate. God is the author of my life. I'm here to encourage you no matter how many hurdles you face. God will be there at the end, holding his hand out to get you across the finish line.

See now that I am He! There is no God besides me. I put to death, and I bring to life, I have wounded, and I will heal, and no one can deliver out of my hand.

-Deuteronomy 32:39

About Shaday

Shaday's life is a testament to living in God's will, encouraging others to nurture their gifts and embrace their unique purpose.

Shaday Void is a Brooklyn Native born July 11, 1989 that channels divine inspiration into her craft. Celebrating her gift for writing and crafting through singing and praise dancing in her apartment.

Adoring purple and pineapple, she carefully crafts soaps for her business Love is Sweet Soaps and has authored two children's books; both available on Amazon. "Love Made a Family" and "Share My Hair."

Stay connected to Shaday on Facebook @shadaydiy

The Call That Changed Everything
Dr. Leticia Perry Warren

I received a phone call that forever changed my life on November 20, 2023. On the other end of the phone was a law enforcement officer. He began to ask me if I was Leticia. Yes, I replied. He began to tell me that my mother was in a bad accident and that I needed to come to the hospital immediately. I asked the officer if my mother was okay. He told me she was alert and orientated. My response was okay, thank you, Lord, and I felt deep relief as I hung up the phone.

Approximately 2 minutes later, the phone rang again. It was the same officer calling, but this time, the tone of his voice had changed. His instruction was due to the severity of the injury to your mother's leg; she had to be airlifted to another hospital. At this time, I felt like something was not right. Therefore, I asked the officer, "If it's just a leg injury, why is she being airlifted to another hospital?" He explained that the hospital they are sending her to is better equipped to handle severe cases. I said okay, but I still had an unsettled feeling within. I told my daughter something was not right.

As we got closer to the hospital, I experienced so much anxiety. As we arrived there, I told the ER receptionist that my mother had been airlifted to this hospital and gave her name. The staff took me and my daughter to this little conference room. I felt like I could not breathe. I told my daughter; okay, I know something is not right. I work at the hospital, and this procedure is done when someone has passed away or coded in which they are in critical condition. All kinds of thoughts bombarded my mind. I tried to pray, but I was overwhelmed by my emotions.

My daughter said maybe they had to take her for emergency surgery. I said, okay, I pray you are right. I begin to talk to the Lord, asking him to settle me. As I calmed down, three hospital staff came into the conference room dressed in regular clothing. One of the staff asked us, "Were we the family of Joanne Williams?" Yes, I replied, I am her daughter, and she began to ask me what I knew concerning my mother being in an accident. Now I am looking at her like, what kind of crazy question is this? Tell me what you know.

Of course, I had to dismiss that thought. I began to tell her that I was told my mother had been in a bad accident. Her fiancé' did not make it, but she did. She was airlifted to this hospital because of the severe injury to her leg. At this time, the other staff member, who was the chaplain, said, "Leticia, we are sorry your mother did not make it." At this time, it seemed as if the room was closing in on me, and I couldn't breathe. The last thing I remember saying is, are you sure before hitting the floor? The nurse went to get the doctor to talk to me and my daughter. It felt like someone had punched me in my stomach and left me grasping for breath. At this point, I couldn't understand how my mother went from being alert and talking to no longer being here.

During this experience, I learned that the Lord will give you the power to get up. I got up to walk down this long hall to see my mother for the last time. I begin to ask the Lord, how do I accept this? What do I do with all this hurt and pain from this traumatic experience? He tells me to grieve the right way to be healed and made whole. But first, you must forgive the person that caused the accident. At that moment, I forgave that person. From that moment forward, the Lord took me on a journey that would teach me how not to let the nature of grief take root in me to hold me captive. The complete journey is in my new book, "Breaking the Chains of Grief."

About Dr. Leticia

Dr. Leticia Perry is the wife of Willie B. Perry. She is the daughter of George Watson and Joanne Williams (Warren). She is a mother of three and a grandmother.

In addition, she is a servant, exhorter, motivator, author, certified and trained Christian life and mental health coach, mental health advocate, and entrepreneur. Leticia Perry is a Licensed, Ordained Pastor with a Doctorate of Christian Theology. The Lord has anointed her to proclaim the Good News to those who are bound and broken and to release hope to the discouraged. It is her desire to impact the lives of others through exaltation and motivation.

As a momentum coach, she shares encouraging videos weekly on her Facebook group page, *"Kingdom Inspirations."* As a pastor of Kingdom Works Ministries International Community Church Campus 2, service and community outreach is held in Henderson, North Carolina.

Pastor Leticia's weekly teaching is aired on *"Spreading the Gospel Network Radio,"* which allows her teachings and the gospel to be spread worldwide. Finally, Leticia ministers to the elderly in her community. She works one-on-one with them regarding their spiritual and physical needs. She enjoys spending quality time with her family.

The Secret
SANDRA WASHINGTON

For God shall bring every work into judgment, with every secret thing, whether it be good, or whether it be evil.
Ecclesiastes 12:14 KJV

The secret started on October 22,1962, as that was the day I, Sandra Louise Washington, was born. I am sure I was conceived during a shared love experience with my mom and dad, but still, there was secrecy. Those people in my mom and dad's circle of love knew, but as a baby, no one told me. Later, when I learned the truth, I asked my mom about this secret and why it had been kept a secret for so long.

She explained to me the circumstances at the time and why a nurse who was a stranger in the hospital where I was born told her to do what she did. I understood her reasoning, but I still had and continue to have thoughts on why the secret was never correctly fixed when I was a young girl. However, I've guessed that my dad passing away when I was a toddler was the reason why she did not follow through on bringing the secret out for all to know.

My thoughts often lead me to the fact that she was protecting me from receiving ostracizing remarks, and she was also protecting her own heart and mind. She had to have known that eventually, I would learn the truth, and then she would have the mother-and-daughter talk that we had when I confronted her.

The second secret started when I was a young girl, and I have lived with that secret for over 20 years. This secret should never have happened, but it did repeatedly. Instead of sharing my secret, I lived with it and let it drive me to the point of being labeled lazy, a militant, and a wild child. I blamed the adults for not knowing something was wrong for a long time.

As I think about why I did not say anything, I am not sure why I did not tell my mother what was happening to me once she dropped me off at my grandparents' house so I could be looked after while she went to work. I remember being sworn to secrecy during the times of molestation, and I remember receiving money and other gifts for keeping that secrecy. I knew my young mind and body were being shredded and ripped into pieces.

My attitude towards schoolwork and towards making friends soured. I began hanging out at all the wrong places, running away from home, and not going to see my nanny became a constant. Most of my teen years and my adult years were spent wilding out. I dated numerous men who I knew were no good for me; I was almost raped (thank God for the Good Samaritan). I suffered from a sense of being an outcast; you name it, everything that could go right, I made sure went wrong.

The secret I kept to myself was driving me to the point of no return. Yet, this person who was responsible for my misery was living as if he did nothing wrong. His church members admired him as a great Deacon; everyone who knew him looked up to him.
Add to that the fact that when I was growing up, I did not have a close relationship with the paternal side of my family but instead spent a significant amount of time with my sisters and their paternal side of the family. This is not to say that I did not know the paternal side of my family, as I was aware of some of them, but not all.

Whatever the reason, I spent more time around my sisters' family. They made me feel welcome whenever I was around, but one night, while I was in my early twenties, a statement made me feel like a total outcast. Once again, I held on to the secret that I had, but I made mental plans to escape from the nightmare that I had been living since I was a young girl.

I began daydreaming about having someone from my dad's family come to the rescue. Realizing that would not happen, I let my life spiral out of control. Then I found out that I was pregnant. I had a baby growing inside of me that would require my full attention. I had to make a choice about what to do with a baby when, internally, I was still holding on to a secret.

During my pregnancy, I decided to share my secret with someone close to me. Thus, I told my older sister. I told her I was able to release the genie from the bottle. She listened as I told her about what happened. I felt some relief but not entirely because I expected her to tell the remainder of my family; however, she chose to remain silent. I believe the reason she took this secret to her grave is because she wanted me to tell my story. I miss her dearly now and often picture her telling me she was uncomfortable repeating my story. I can hear her whispering that the story was mine to tell. As I write this, I can hear her whispering that she did not tell my story as it was not hers to tell.

After sharing the secret with my sister and giving birth to a baby boy, I began foolishly thinking that the nightmares and thoughts that would constantly remind me of what I had gone through as a young girl would stop only; they did not. They kept coming with a fierceness, especially after my son was diagnosed with a heart condition that would require extensive medical care. I could not help but blame myself for his heart condition. I would consistently question myself whether the secret that I had held inside had anything to do with what, at that time, seemed like a curse that was then harming my son.

Sensing something was wrong and not wanting my life or that of my son's to be in a harmful way, my sisters and my mother stepped in and up and smothered the both of us with love and attention. Neither my sisters nor my mother had any idea of the mental turmoil I was going through. There was no way that my sister had any idea of the turmoil I was going through as I did not tell her. I only told her what happened.

Jeremiah 29:11
 For I know the plans I have for you," declares the Lord, "plans to prosper you and not to harm you, plans to give you hope and a future.

Running away is how I thought I could make the nightmares of molestation go away. Thus, I boarded a plane and moved me and my son eight hundred miles away from family and friends to a place where I only knew a handful of people. I did not realize when I made that move that the plans that

God had for me would involve me meeting, dating, and marrying a man who would help me confront my secrets and encourage me to find my paternal family and speak to my mom about what occurred when I was a little girl. He let me know and showed me He would be with me as I let the genie out of the bottle. He waited patiently and allowed me to take my time to tell my mom. He cheered when I located my sister and paternal family through Facebook. He encouraged me to see a mental health therapist and was relieved when I set up an appointment.

I had a conversation with my mom and told her how I felt about growing up with a last name that was not mine, about how my step-grandfather violated me as a young girl, and how that violation led me down all the wrong roads that I went down as a teen and as a woman who was now in her forties. We spoke briefly about why I did not carry my father's last name, and she reminded me of the story she had already shared.

She advised me that it hurt for her to not find out what happened to me until decades after it happened. She asked me when these occurrences happened and why I kept that secret. She thanked me for telling her but shared that she thought it was her fault that I moved so far away from home and often asked God to tell her what she had done to run me away. She asked me why I had not told her what was happening because she said she would have stopped them. She stated that she would not have sent me back into a harmful situation. She thought she was sending me into a safe spot while she worked.

My mother apologized for the experiences in my life that led me in the wrong direction. She was glad I had finally found my voice and shared my secret with her. I vowed to myself and shared with my husband that I would one day tell my story. I would tell it in a way that would give respect and honor to my mom for the incredible single parent mom, who would do and very often did what was in her children's best interest when she knew what they were facing.

She passed away in December of 2023, and while I miss her dearly, I am glad that she could see how God took my crooked path and straightened it into one full of hope and prosperity.

Mark Chapter 5:34 NIV He said to her, "Daughter, your faith has healed you. Go in peace and be freed from your suffering."

At the end of the day, there are no more secrets. I have uncovered the one secret I kept locked inside for so long. The two therapists that I received therapy from helped me to know and understand that what happened was not my fault. I forgive my Step-grandfather in that I know it was a sickness in him that made him do those horrible things, but I will never forget. My faith has truly healed me. I write this for all children, little girls, and boys, who are told never to share something an adult is doing to them. Mom and Dad, encourage your children to tell you all the things that happen to them when they are in the company of adults. Sometimes, secrets must be told.

About Sandra

Sandra L. Washington is a healthcare professional who owns and manages Medi-Helpz LLC. She is also the founder of the C.H.L.M.S Medi-Helpz Foundation and is known for her international speaking engagements and bestselling book. Sandra is an Independent Board-Certified Patient Advocate who helps patients understand the importance of speaking up for themselves. She collaborates with patients, healthcare providers, and businesses to ensure patients receive the best possible care.

Sandra received her Bachelor's degree from DePaul University and her Master's in Public Policy Administration from Northwestern University. She lives in Chicago, Illinois with her husband and has one adult son.

Sandra believes that healthcare disparities in the United States need to be addressed. She advocates for a collective effort involving patients, doctors, technology experts, and policymakers to create a fair and effective healthcare system.

The Women of the Waiting Room Devotional

The Weight of the Past
SIMONE WILLIAMS-YOUNG

Have you ever felt as if you were living life looking from the outside in? It's as if life is going full speed, you know it's you living it but somehow it feels like someone else's life. Well, that was me. From the time I could remember, it felt like I existed but had never truly lived life. I necessarily did not have a bad life. I had two parents who loved me, yet I felt alone. It was as if everyone had told me I mattered, but I never felt I mattered. There was a hole, a void, and you can even say a disconnect that I did not know how to fix.

I was a sheltered child. My parents were a little overprotective. My mother is a godly woman and had me in church a lot. I was not allowed to listen to secular music or do a lot of the things other children got to do, which most times made me feel awkward, naïve, and just strange. I could not identify with other children my age because I led a sheltered life. The only time I felt a sense of normality was when I went to my father's house, I got to watch music videos and be so excited to go to school the next day and tell someone I heard or saw something current, and then finally I could connect with my peers until that got old and had nothing else in common.

As I got older, the void and the voices in my head grew, too. The voices were telling me that I wasn't worth anything and that the only good things about me were my looks and body, and I listened to the voices. Boys my age, even grown men, started to notice me, and I developed an alter ego to make myself okay with the attention. I no longer felt isolated or like the awkward kid; I felt like I had a place in this world somewhat, and I was okay with that for a while. I sought validation from men, but that got me nowhere. I had a baby at 19, then another child at 20. By the time I had my second child, the voices started to get loud again because of the embarrassment of having another child out of wedlock. I was so depressed that I often thought of committing suicide while pregnant. I hated myself and felt so worthless and useless. I started feeding into the fact that whatever I got from men, I deserved and that no one would truly love me.

During that time, I thought about having an abortion because the shame was unbearable. One Sunday, I went to a church, and the guest pastor who spoke said, "There is someone in here that's about to do something that you know you should not be doing, and God said Don't do it!" I knew that he was talking about me. I had an appointment set up and everything for that week. They were going to have to surgically remove my child because I was later in the pregnancy than a normal abortion. Right there, I started wailing from the pit of my stomach because I knew God was talking to me. God had shown up for me because he knew I was not in my right mind, but I knew his voice. I ended up bringing in a beautiful baby boy who I ended up having a special bond with until his passing in 2020 from gun violence.

From there, I got married and had 3 children. We were married for 17 years. This marriage mentally almost broke me. He was an alcoholic, and towards the end of our marriage, it was like living with a person with multiple personalities. I stayed because I felt I deserved the punishment. When I had my bridal shower, God sent a prophet who stood boldly before everyone there and said," God, said "This is not the man that I have for you. Still, because you want him, I will give you the desires of your heart. But if you do marry him you will stay on your face in my face!" meaning I would stay constantly in prayer because this man was not meant for me. I married him anyway. We already had a son together, and my oldest two children's father was not in their lives, which I always felt guilty about. I refused to let this one grow up without a father in his life, so I married him even though I was warned, and it almost cost me my sanity.

Later, God led me to a church where I grew more spiritually. I started to learn more about who I was in Him. For the first time in my life, I found my identity. I no longer had to accept what men gave me to fill a void? When the voices tried to find their way, I learned how to fight in the spirit against it. I learned how to face my fears and got my divorce because I was scared to divorce him. I learned how to love myself, flaws and all. I learned to work on the things about me that I did not like instead of beating myself up about it. Once I learned how to truly love myself, God blessed me with the love of my life. My now husband sees and knows the real me. You see, the voices were wrong. There is someone out there who loves me, but I could not get him until I learned how to be free of the past and forgive myself. I did not think I was smart, but now I have several businesses. I am more than just my body. I am the daughter of the King.

My waiting room experience was a journey of healing and restoration, Re-evaluation of self-worth, rediscovery of strength, renewed faith and hope, and empowerment and self-care. None of this could have been done without developing a close relationship with God and relying on him.

About Simone

Simone Williams-Young can be described as a Dream and Vision encourager. She is a book publisher, entrepreneur, prophet, mentor, author, wife, grandmother, and, most importantly, a servant of the Most High God. Her goal is to inspire people to reach toward everything that God has in store for them.

She is also the author of three books titled "The Chain Breaking Experience: Poetry Devotional Book", *"Stronger, Better, Wiser: Walk Into the New You!"* and "I Choose to Live: Pushing Through the Grieving Process." This book is a personal testimony of how she overcame the loss of her son, who was killed in his prime by gun violence.

Contact Information:

FB- Author Simone Williams-Young, Simone Williams

Email: contact@Yahpublishingllc.com

Website: linktr.ee/SimoneWilliamsYoung

Worry, A Suitcase Made of Thorns
LaQuita Parks

What would you do if your four-year-old daughter said she was worried about passing the physics class when she entered medical school? Would that cause you to worry? What about if your nine-year-old couldn't sleep at night because he was worried if there would be any social security for him and his friends when they turn seventy? Would you be worried then? How about if your seven-year-old is worried about what kind of parent she will be, and her face is stressed. What would be your response be to the worry of such young minds? Maybe you would call the child psychologist.

Perhaps you are blessed not to have such worries in life. Or, as an adult, you may have a bevy of other stressful, can't sleep, mind-altering things that cause a raging storm in your heart.

I don't know what you may be worried about; however, if you are a child of the King, your worries are over, and you can rest in the stillness of peace. The Psalmist said, "He leadeth me beside the still waters" (23:2).

The word "leadeth" in the KJV coveys the idea of a continuous, never-ending act. "Still waters" is a reference to repose in peacefulness, a quiet, restful place. Worry can be described as a suitcase made of thorns. Packed in it are "what-ifs" and "how-wills."

What if I choose the wrong relationship?

What if it rains?

What if something goes wrong?

How will I pay for this car?

How will I find a job?

This suitcase does not have graspable handles. It's cumbersome, bulky, and ugly—so ugly that no one offers to carry it, and you really don't want to carry it either.

The biblical word for worry is actually two Greek words: "Merrizo," to divide, and "nous," the mind. Worry divides the mind. It causes a separation between today's priorities and tomorrow's problems. Part of our mind is on the present, and the other part is on the not now. The result is half-minded peace or no peace.

So what are we to do?

Jesus said, "Take no thought (be not anxious) for your life," concerning the necessities of life because your life is deeper than those physical things (Matt.6:25). Jesus said don't allow your thoughts to be divided between the physical things of life over against the spiritual things (v33).

"First" means in order of importance. All of us recognize and realize what "first" means. It does not mean next, second, or last. Someone often says, "He or she was first in their class." Immediately, we understand what "first" means. Therefore, it's not a stretch to understand what Jesus means when he speaks of the first things we should seek.

Frets are futile and faithless. Worry has never made a gray hair black, a short person tall, a skinny person fat, a broke person rich, healed a broken relationship, cured a disease, or brought a wayward child home.

I once heard a story (I don't know if it's true) about a man who worried so much that he hired someone to worry for him. He said he would pay him 300K a year to worry for him. The man asked where he would get the money to pay him. The man told him, that's not my worry, that's yours.

Since it's impossible to "will" worry to others or to pay someone to worry for us, what should we do?

David had the answer by recognizing the one who led him. There are two things we can't do simultaneously: lead and follow. Either the Shepherd will lead the sheep or the sheep will be lost.

"He leads me" means the Shepherd is not behind me telling me where to go. He is in front like a guide on an African safari, clearing and cutting a path for me to walk freely through. We sing, "He leadeth me," yet we fail to follow. Isaiah writes that God leads thee by the path that thy shall go (48:17).

The Shepherd is aware of the minefields on the narrow road. He tells us when and where to turn (GPS). He warns us where the precipices are located. Like a guide for a blind person, He tells us when to step up or down. Just like the GPS knows when and what to tell us ahead of time so that we can prepare for the next thing on the road, the Shepherd leads us in the same manner. The writer of Hebrews says that (4:16). The Shepherd always helps us in time.

Jesus sent His disciples out to teach the gospel and told them not to be concerned about what they would need (Mk.13:11). God provided manna for Israel daily. God always does the right thing at the right time. Knowing that the Shepherd's provision is timely, we can rest in continuous peace in the present.

"Take therefore no thought for the morrow: for the morrow shall take thought for the things of itself. Sufficient unto the day *is* the evil thereof "(Matt.6:34). Pay close attention to the last phrase. "I have no idea what I will do if..." you will when the time comes. The "ifs" happened, the child died, left home, went to jail, got pregnant, the spouse cheated and left, lost a job, the parents died, the best friend became a worse enemy, etc.

I could never teach a Bible class, speak at a function, or be a team leader. All this may be true if you try to know everything at once. When the time comes, you will know...at that time. The key is to meet today's problem with today's strength. Don't pull tomorrow's problems over today's present problems. Tomorrow's strength will come tomorrow. Use today's strength for today's task.

Therefore, Jesus tells us to leave tomorrow's problem in tomorrow. God is leading you. Sometimes, we are so worried that sleep escapes us. We try to count sheep, and it does not work. Stop counting sheep and read about the Shepherd who leads the sheep to still waters so that they can lie down to sleep in perfect peace.

The Shepherd gives us His promise in His word to be a lamp unto our feet and a light to guide our feet. When we have the peace of God, we can enjoy peace with God.

About LaQuita

LaQuita Parks is the Founder and CEO of Pa-Pro-Vi Publishing and A Failure 2 Communicate LLC as well as a Relationship Communication Coach, Writing Coach and Mentor with a passion for people and their well-being. She is also the host of her own podcast show, "My Heart on Pages" and the host of "The Power of YOUR Story" radio show. LaQuita is also the Founder and Facilitator of EXHALE-a social communication group for women who meet to discuss different issues, ranging from personal to political.

Walking Limitations is LaQuita's first published book and the true story of how she went into the hospital to have a simple procedure and it left her crippled for life at the hands of a nurse. This created a medical tsunami that has affected her life for the last forty-nine years.

LaQuita created the Pa-Pro-Vi Publishing platform to help people start the healing process because she believes there is power in YOUR story and that writing and sharing your story can be therapeutic. Since starting Pa-Pro-Vi Publishing in 2020, LaQuita has been able to help clients all over the country take their stories from a "thought to a realization."

LaQuita also has a degree in Business and has been planning and facilitating successful mentoring and communication coaching sessions for nearly twenty years throughout the State of Georgia and in Duluth, Minnesota

LaQuita is a faithful Christian who enjoys teaching bible study. She was baptized into Christ in 2008. She is a mother of three adult children and Nanna to 5 little heartbeats. LaQuita is a self-published author of several books including her semi autobiography titled Walking Limitations by Other People's Definition, and two children's books, she has also been featured in various magazines, and interviewed on numerous TV Networks, radio, and podcast platforms. In June 2023, she became a #1 International Best-Selling Author as a part of a book project called "My Two Cents on Self-Love. LaQuita lives in Riverdale, Ga and has been a member of the Forest Park Church of Christ Congregation since 2008.

Connect with LaQuita:

Facebook: https://www.facebook.com/laquita.parks.3/

Instagram: https://www.instagram.com/paprovipublishing/

Twitter: https://twitter.com/AFTC_LaQuita

Linked In: https://www.linkedin.com/in/laquita-parks-a03647a/

Website: https://paprovipublishing.com/

Email: laquita@afailure2communicate.com

paprovipublishing@yahoo.com

Power of Prayer

Heavenly Father,

We come before You today with humble hearts, recognizing that You are the creator of all things and the source of eternal life. We acknowledge that we have wrestled with our own desires and struggled to fully surrender our lives to You. But we know that You are patient and loving, waiting for us to be ready to obey Your will.

Lord, we ask that You reveal to us the incredible plans You have for our lives as we release words of faith and trust in Your power. Help us to understand that You are not limited by our circumstances or struggles, but that You are always with us, ready to work miracles in our lives.

For all those who have purchased the paperback, hard copy, or e-book of "Listen Linda Presents The Women of the Waiting Room Surgery for Your Soul," we invite them to raise their right hand unto You as a symbol of their surrender and commitment to You. May this act of surrender be a powerful moment of transformation in their lives.

Father, we pray that as readers and co-authors and anyone else who has played a part in spreading this message and engage with this book, both in the devotional and anthology sections, it will touch their hearts and inspire them to commit their lives to You and Jesus Christ. Let the words written within these pages penetrate their souls, bringing them closer to You and igniting a fire within them to live a life devoted to Your purpose.

We thank You, Lord, for the gift of salvation through Jesus Christ. We believe that He is the Son of God, that He died on the cross for our sins, and that on the third day He rose again, conquering death so that we can have eternal life. Today, we invite You, Lord, to come into our hearts, to forgive us of our sins, and to live Your life in us and through us.

From this day forward, our lives belong to You, Lord. We surrender ourselves completely to Your will and ask that You guide us every step of the way. Help us to walk in obedience, to trust in Your plan, and to live a life that brings glory to Your name.

In Jesus' name, we pray. Amen.

May this prayer resonate deeply within the hearts of all who read it, leading them to a closer relationship with You, Lord. May it be a catalyst for transformation and a reminder of Your unfailing love and grace.

The Women of the Waiting Room Devotional

www.ingramcontent.com/pod-product-compliance
Lightning Source LLC
Chambersburg PA
CBHW072133160426
43197CB00012B/2084